# A Reading
# of
# Feminist Literature

# A Reading of Feminist Literature

*Edited by*
**R.K. Dhawan**
**Meeta Shukla**

**Prestige Books International**
New Delhi

*Published by*
**Prestige Books International**
New Delhi 110 060
prestigebooks@gmail.com
Phone: 9818755529

*Associate Office*
11B, Broomwood Road
London SW11 6HU

*Associate Office*
P.O. Box 2250
Sydney 2001


ISBN: 978-81-938503-6-7



Printed in India

# Contents

## Pakistan and Bangladesh

## Canada and America



## Book Review

# Creative Writing

# A Reading of Feminist Literature
# Introduction

**R.K. DHAWAN** and **MEETA SHUKLA**

What is feminist literature? How do we define it? Feminist literature, by common consent, is fiction, non-fiction, poetry or drama that supports the feminist goals of defining and advocating equal civil, political and social rights for women. At the core of feminist sociology is the idea of the systemic oppression of women and the domination of men in society. The protest addressed as Feminism has been used as an umbrella term to describe those who felt the need to oppose the suppression of women on social and ideological grounds. As a discipline, Feminist criticism does not exist in isolation. It draws upon various schools of thought such as Marxism, Structuralism, Existentialism, Deconstruction and so on. This is evident in the various approaches adopted by critics during the last five decades. Contemporary feminism celebrates the womenfolk who enjoy economic independence and also share the responsibilities of life with the opposite gender.

The present volume offers feminist literary criticism, informed by feminist theory, broadly speaking, by the politics of feminism. It uses the principles and ideology of feminism to critique the language of literature. Feminist literary criticism seeks to examine texts within literary canon through a new lense. It is interesting to note that feminist criticism has not emerged all of a sudden; its history is extensive, from classic works of nineteenth-century writers like George Eliot to the current "third-wave" authors. For the feminists, the text is a battleground where actual power relations between men and women are played out.

An offshoot of Feminism is the emergence of Lesbian and Gay theories. The discipline of literary theories in the past focussed mainly on the issues of gender, race and class. There was however a curious silence on the matters of non-heterosexual relations; those with sexual preference 'outside' the heterosexual were relegated to the background. Lesbianism emerged primarily as a political and social movement. Queer theory is thus the byproduct of the alliance between gay and lesbian theories and sociology.

There was a time when Indian women would silently weep on their pillows after a violent row with their husbands. But not anymore. They refuse to take things lying down. They take on their abusive husbands head on, legally or at times drawing them out of their hideouts. Thanks to the feminist movement, Indian women now have the guts and will to walk out of their painful lives. Earlier, a lot of women had a lurking fear as to what would become of them if they walk out of marriage. They were submerged with guilt at having to burden their parents, hoping that their life would change one day perhaps. They experienced low self-esteem that kept them subdued and diffident. They feared a split would cause a disaster.

Women have started coming out of shell, actively participating in the mainstream life. Today, nobody has a problem with a woman working, but every woman invariably faces casual sexism at work. Recently, the movement #MeToo has been propped up by women who have taken up the cudgels against men who sexually exploit women. This has supported and empowered their lives and careers and brought them together in fighting against misconduct of men.

One of the most challenging aspects of sexual harassment is dealing with the grey areas between coercion and consent. Such allegations remain complex issues where it has not been easy to deliver judgement. Was it a rape or a matter of mutual consent? But why did she not complain earlier? If she did not complain earlier; the insinuation was that it was a figment of her imagination. This was in line with the response of the perpetrators who denied that such an incident had taken place. Women have started to stand up against gender biases but the world is still not able to digest their being vocal about their choices.

The volume attempts to examine a few contemporary writers who directly or indirectly have engaged themselves in the vital task of formulating a new consciousness about women in the fast-changing environment today. These writers have focussed on women's quest for self-identity, emancipation and revolt against chauvinistic tradition. In their creative writing, there has emerged the image of new woman with feminist consciousness and capacity to face the crisis boldly. This collection of critical essays helps us to establish the positive role of the novelists in English in the vital ongoing battle of establishing female selfhood.

# Feminism: Role in Literature

**JYOTI YADAV**
**Sri Ram Institute of Teacher Education, I.P. University**
**SANGEETA KUMARI**
**Student, Maharishi Dayanand University, Rohtak**

Simone de Beauvoir has given a full-length commentary on the plight of women today. It is worthwhile to quote the author on this subject: "The women of today are in a fair way to dethrone the myth of feminity, they are beginning to affirm their independence in concrete ways; but they do not easily succeed in living completely to lift a human being. Reared by women, which still means practically subordination to man; for masculine prestige is far from extinction, resting still, on economic and social foundation."

Simone de Beauvoir wrote that "the first time we see a woman take up her pen in defence of her sex" was Christine de Pizan who wrote *Epitre au Dieu d'Amour* (Epistle to the God of Love) in the 15th century. Heinrich Cornelius Agrippa and Modesta di Pozzo di Forzi worked in the 16th century. Marie Le Jars de Gournay, Anne Bradstreet and Francois Poullain de la Barre wrote during the 17th century.

First-wave feminism refers to an extended period of feminist activity during the nineteenth century and early twentieth century in the United Kingdom and the United States. It refers mainly to the women's suffrage movement. Originally it focused on the promotion of equal contract and property rights for women and the opposition to chattel marriage and ownership of married women (and their children) by their husbands. The first main figure of feminism was the 18th century British writer Mary Wollstonecraft. However, by the end of the nineteenth century, activism focused primarily on gaining political power, particularly the right of women's suffrage.

American first-wave feminism involved a wide range of women. Some, such as Frances Willard, belonged to conservative Christian groups such as the Woman's Christian Temperance Union. Others, such as Matilda Joslyn Gage, were more radical, and expressed themselves within the National Woman Suffrage Association or individually. John Stuart Mill later brought the idea of women's suffrage up in his election platform of 1865 and was later joined by many men and women fighting for the same cause. American first-wave feminism is considered to have ended with the passage of the Nineteenth Amendment to the United States Constitution (1919), granting women the right to vote in all states.

The term first wave was coined retrospectively after the term second-wave feminism began to be used to describe a newer feminist movement that focused as much on fighting social and cultural inequalities as political inequalities. It refers to a period of feminist activity from mid-1960s through late 1970s and it is associated with the women's liberation movements.

The feminist activist and author Carol Hanisch coined the slogan "The Personal is Political" which became synonymous with the second wave. Second-wave feminists saw women's cultural and political inequalities inextricably linked and encouraged women to understand aspects of their personal lives as deeply politicized and as reflecting sexist power structures.

Betty Friedan's *The Feminine Mystique* (1963) criticized the idea that women could only find fulfilment through child-rearing and home-making. According to Friedan's obituary in the *New York Times*, *The Feminine Mystique* "ignited the contemporary women's movement in 1963 and as a result permanently transformed the social fabric of the United States and countries around the world" and "is widely regarded as one of the most influential non-fiction books of the 20th century." In the book Friedan hypothesizes that women are victims of a false belief system that requires them to find identity and meaning in their lives through their husbands and children. Such a system causes women to completely lose their identity in that of their family.

It began in early 1990 arising as a response to proved failures of second wave. It highlighted the focus on queer and non-white women. Third-wave feminism also contains internal debates between different feminists such as the psychologist Carol Gilligan (who believes that there are important differences between the sexes) and those who believe that there are no inherent differences between the sexes and contend that gender roles are due to social conditioning.

Rethinking society with feminist theory was accomplished by, among other disciplines, women's studies, feminist literary criticism, gynocriticism, socialist feminism and the feminist art movement. Looking through a feminist lens at history, politics, culture and economics, feminists developed insights in just about every intellectual discipline.

Sometimes, situation is not good and women take decision of abortion but it is not legal; this rule can create a problem for her. The call for "abortion on demand" is often misunderstood. Leaders of the women's liberation movement were clear that women should have reproductive freedom and safe access to legal abortion, making the choice for her reproductive status without interference by the state or paternalistic medical professionals because women know what is right for her.

Feminists helped spark debate over assumptions embedded in our language that reflects the assumption of a male-dominated patriarchal society. Language was often centred on males, assuming that humanity was male; women were only exceptions. Use neutral pronouns? Identify words with gender bias? Invent new words? Many solutions were tried for "De-Sexing the English Language."

Education for women is important because it is her right. Many women went to college and worked professionally in the early 20th century, but the mid-century myth of the middle-class suburban housewife downplayed the importance of women's education. Feminists knew that girls and women must be encouraged to seek an education, and not just as "something to fall back on," if they were to become, and be seen as, "fully" equal.

Feminists worked for the Equal Rights Amendment, the Equal Pay Act, and the addition of sex discrimination to the Civil Rights Act and other laws that would guarantee equality. Feminists advocated for a variety of laws and interpretations of existing laws to remove impediments to women's professional and economic achievements, or full exercise of citizenship rights (such as having women on juries on an equal basis). Feminists questioned the long tradition of "protective legislation" for women which often ended up sidelining women from being hired, promoted, or treated fairly.

The League of Women Voters had existed since women won the right to vote, and the LWV had supported educating women (and men) in informed voting, and had done some work in promoting women as candidates. In the 1960s and 1970s, other organizations were created and the LWV extended its mission to promote more participation in the political process by women including recruiting, training and financially supporting women candidates.

In a nuclear family, a woman's role is important; she plays many roles. Although not all feminists called for collective mothering or went so far as to urge "seizing the means of reproduction," as Shulamith Firestone wrote in *The Dialectic of Sex*, it was clear that women should not have to bear the sole responsibility for raising children. Supporting women as parents, feminism re-examined the maternal role expected of women. Feminism also worked to support women when they were the primary caretakers of children or the primary custodial parents. They give their best time for their kids. Feminists worked for family leave, employment rights through pregnancy and childbirth including covering pregnancy and newborn medical expenses through health insurance, child-care, and reform in marriage and divorce laws.

"I Want a Wife," this essay in the first issue of Ms. magazine meant that every woman literally wanted a wife, but it did suggest that any adult would love to have someone to play the "housewife" role as it had been defined.

The novelist has described a few other situations to prove that people were tired of their class and occasionally they enjoyed an interaction with members of the other classes. Shobha De portrays through her characters the metropolitan social life and cultural cross-fertilization. However, the novelist cannot restrain from writing about the problematic lives of Indian women residing in the metropolis. Shobha De's observation coheres with Cora Kaplan who claims, "Literature has been a traditional space for the exploration of gender relations and sexual difference, and one in which women themselves have been formidably present."

Though a lot has changed in today's time, there is still an underlying wave of feminism, the presence of which one can sense all over the world. While in the urban setting, women have almost been given their dues, in the rural setting, women are still expected to live by the stereotypes cast by society. Even in the urban setting, though women have achieved a lot more than society has given them credit for, they are still expected to fulfill certain roles and stereotypes that have been the norm for centuries. Feminist literature of different periods will depict different desires and different wants under the purview of feminism. The roles of daughters, wives, and mothers in literature will keep changing, and so will their requirements and beliefs. The concept of gender equality that focuses primarily on women's rights has come a long way, and feminist literature has been a great medium to bring about any visible changes in the attitude towards women. Yet, it is a long battle that is being fought, and it will be a while before gender equality and the role of women in society will be clear in the ideal sense.

# Feminism in the Light of Transnationalism

**PRIYA KULKARNI**
**Bankatlal Badruka College for Info. Tech., Hyderabad**

The term feminism can be used to describe a political, cultural or economic movement aimed at establishing more rights and legal protection for women. Feminism involves political and sociological theories and philosophies concerned with issues of gender difference, as well as a movement that advocates more gender-specific rights for women and campaigns for women's rights and interests. But the gender originates in objective biological specifies of the two sexes in terms of the roles each is expected to play.

How far the people justify the feminism practically. Feminism literally means advocacy of women's rights on the ground of equality between men and women, socially, politically and economically. But inequality is still ruling the male-dominated society.

A famous English writer and one of the foremost modernists of the twentieth century Virginia Woolf's writes: "As a woman I have no country. As a woman my country is the whole world." In this world, every human being has equal right to live, the word 'human being' is applicable to both men and women.

The term "feminism" originated from the French word "feminisme," coined by the utopian socialist Charles Fourier, and was first used in English in the 1890s, in association with the movement for equal political and legal rights for women. Feminism takes a number of forms in a variety of disciplines such as feminist geography, feminist history and feminist literary criticism.

Geraldine Ferraro, the first woman to be nominated as Vice-President of the United States, said: "We've chosen the path to equality, don't let them turn us around." Constance Baker Motley, the first Black Woman in the U.S. to become a Federal Judge, said: "Something which we think is impossible now is not impossible in another decade."

The history of feminism can sum up both success and failure of feminism of past. I want to go with success to gain strength to make the past failure as success in the modern era. The history of feminism narrates the movements and ideologies aimed at equal rights for women. While the roots of feminism are buried in ancient Greece, most recognize the movement by the three waves of feminism.

The first wave of Women's movement was in 1830s to early 1900s. Often taken for granted, women in the late 19th to early 20th centuries realized that they must first gain political power (including the right to vote) to bring about change. Their political agenda expanded to issues concerning sexual, reproductive and economic matters. The seed was planted that women have the potential to contribute just as much if not more than men.

Coming on the heels of World War II, the second wave of feminism (1960s-1980s) focused on the workplace, sexuality, family and reproductive rights. During a time when the United States was already trying to restructure itself, it was perceived that women had met their equality goals with the exception of the failure of the ratification of the Equal Rights Amendment.

The third wave of Women's movement started in 1990s. Today and unlike the former movements, the term 'feminist' is received less critically by the female population due to the varying feminist outlooks. There are the ego-cultural feminists, the radicals, the liberal reforms, the electoral, academic, eco-feminists.

Jane Austen writes, "I hate to hear you talk about all women as if they were fine ladies instead of rational creatures. None of us want to be in calm waters all our lives." This shows that the feminists are fighting since decades for their rights and a true understanding of the term 'feminism.

The main issues faced today were prefaced by the work done by the previous feminists. We are still working to vanquish the disparities in male and female pay and the reproductive rights of women. We are working to end violence against women.

Mary Wollstonecraft (1759-1797) was an English writer and feminist philosopher who raised her voice for gender equality. She lived and wrote at the tail end of the Age of Enlightenment. The ideals of humanism and natural rights at the time were only being applied to men; consider the American Revolution, which established that only men had the right to vote.

Her most famous work, *A Vindication for the Rights of Women*, is one of the pillars of feminism and the women's equality movement. In this book she described the state of ignorance in which society kept women. She also pleaded for better educational opportunities. Her work dealt with expanding the idea of individual liberties of women. She supported herself entirely on her own as her abusive father squandered the family wealth before she came of age. Her life and work remain a tremendous influence today.

American publisher Katherine Graham was the first female CEO of a Fortune 500 company in history. Following the death of her husband and *Washington Post* president, Philip Graham in 1962, Katherine took the reins of the paper. She ascended to de facto publisher in 1963, president in 1967, official publisher in 1969, CEO in 1972, and held the title 'Chairwoman of the Board' from 1973-1997.

As the first and only female Fortune 500 CEO, Graham often felt that she had no role models to look up to. She also felt that many of her male staffers and competitors did not respect her because she was a woman. Her ascension to power coincided with the Women's Liberation movement and she took it upon herself to promote gender equality at the newspaper. In 1997, she published her memoir, *Personal History*, which won the Pulitzer Prize in 1998. She won numerous honours and is considered to be one of America's greatest publishers in the 20th century.

Elizabeth Blackwell achieved the distinction of becoming the first female to earn a medical degree in the United States. Born in England, she moved to America at the age of 11 when her father emigrated to fight for the abolition of slavery. After studying medicine independently for one year, she applied to numerous medical schools in Philadelphia and New York. She was accepted by Geneva Medical College in western New York. During her career she also worked with other female doctors and wrote numerous books including *Medicine as a Profession for Women* in 1860, *Address on the Medical Education of Women* in 1864 and *Pioneer Work in Opening the Medical Profession to Women* in 1895.

Susan Brownell Anthony (1820-1906) was one of the foremost leaders of the American suffragist movement and the anti-slavery movement. She organized numerous campaigns and lectures on the issue all over the country. She was instrumental in forming the Women's Loyal National League, which supported the policies of President Abraham Lincoln. She, along with fifteen other women, voted in the presidential election of 1872, for which she was arrested and convicted. She also co-authored three volumes of History of Woman Suffrage. She was the first woman to be depicted on a U.S coin.

Susan B. Anthony says: "The day will come when men will recognize woman as his peer, not only at the fireside, but in councils of the nation. Then, and not until then, will there be the perfect comradeship, the ideal union between the sexes that shall result in the highest development of the race." The earlier feminists hoped that a day will come when everyone will bury the inequality and gender differences. "No man or woman should depend upon another for maintenance and necessaries. Family discord and social degradation will never end till each depends upon herself."

Anandibai Gopalrao Joshi (31 March 1865-26 February 1887) was one of the first South Asian female physicians and first lady doctor of India. She was the first female of Indian origin to study and graduate with a degree in medicine in the United States. She is also believed to be the first Hindu woman to set foot on American soil.

Women have held important leadership positions and thrived in them. The lives and struggles of women in power provide great insights into what it takes to overcome traditional barriers to women's leadership.

Feminism has changed aspects of Western society. Feminist political activists have been concerned with issues such as individual autonomy, political rights, social freedom, economic independence, abortion and reproductive rights, divorce, workplace rights (including maternity leave and equal pay), and education; and putting an end to domestic violence, gender stereotypes, discrimination, sexism, objectification, and prostitution.

So many women today feel like they have equal opportunities as men. These feminists working in all areas have to negotiate the ways which help to represent new subjectivities including feminist subjectivities.

The most extraordinary initiative which is very close to every woman's heart today is one-third reservation for women in professional education. As its result, women are able to dominate sectors like financial services, health care and information technology, transport and industries, sports, literature and even in entertainment field: it consists of many different segments under its folds such as television, and films.

Women in government in the modern era are under-represented in most countries. Some progress has been made during the last two centuries, women are increasingly being elected to be heads of state and government. On January 2017, the global participation rate of women in national-level parliaments is 23.3%. A number of countries are exploring measures that may increase women's participation in government at all levels, from the local to the national. The U.S presidential election is a recent example. The South African government has produced a number of policies and legislation in pursuit of women's empowerment.

But it doesn't mean that the discrimination has vanished. Even today women are facing many challenges in personal as well as social life. The following situations prompt us to raise our voice against the inequality.

A research study says that only 5% of working women in India make to a senior leadership position in the corporate sector compared to the global average of 20%. Nepal (33%), Pakistan (17.5%), Bangladesh (13%), Peru, Ecuador, Paraguay, France, Portugal, Spain, Sweden (50%), Sudan and Niger have a quota for women in Parliament.

Let us look at influential women in the world today. As First Lady of the United States, a US Senator, and a hugely popular candidate for President of the US, Hillary Clinton has been a trail blazer for women in politics. Having come closer to being nominated for President by a major party than any woman before her, Senator Clinton has encouraged women to join the political process and pursue their dreams.

Indra Krishnamurthy Nooyi (b. 28 October 1955) is an American business executive and the current Chairperson and Chief Executive Officer of PepsiCo, the second largest food and beverage business in the world. She has consistently ranked among the World's 100 Most Powerful Women.

The only woman currently serving on the US Supreme Court, Justice Ginsburg exercises influence over the laws that govern the United States. Like Justice O'Connor before her, Justice Ginsburg helps make the decisions of the highest court in the US, making her not only one of the most influential, but one of the most powerful women in the world. One way her influence can be shown is in the presidential debate: it has been said that whoever becomes president will be pressured to appoint a woman to the Court to replace her when she retires.

Women should be empowered so that they can lead the world to glory. Women play a crucial role in initiating the advancement and growth of any society, in nations across the world.

Women have always stood up for their rights and fought their battles despite restrictions and limitations. They are the shining beacons of hope and have displayed exemplary dedication in their respective fields. Their involvement with public policy at national and International level is a transnational network which is guided by a set of emerging ideas and goals that may be referred to as global feminism.

Government plays a significant role in women development. At the same time, women empowerment should start from home. In every home, women should be encouraged to pursue their passion. In the present era most of women are encouraged to pursue their passion.

# "Sisterhood" in South Asian Women's Writing

**FEROZA JUSSAWALLA**
**University of New Mexico, U.S.A.**

"Sisterhood," has always been a part of Indian culture, despite the many myths of "women against women," in the joint family system. It has been particularly so, in times of emergencies, such as the independence movement, or other times when there have been political upheavals, wars and stressors. It is also true that there has been solidarity among South Asian women writers from the earliest of times, particularly Indian women writers. And women writers have striven to create characters who show solidarity among women. And so we can posit that despite the stereotype of women's oppression in India, or South Asia in general, there has been a tendency towards feminism from the beginnings of Indian writing in English. In this paper, I will not be considering early ancient or medieval Hindu women, goddesses and queens, who have always been portrayed in leadership roles in myths and epics. It is glib for us to simply say, to "foreigners" that Indian women have always had more feminist tendencies, because we can point to Indira Gandhi or Mrs. Bandaranayke. But we can show ordinary women as authors and authors who created characters who exhibit heroism in their day-to-day lives.

First let's look at our history of women writers writing in English. For this I turn to K.R. Srinivasa Iyengar's monumental history of literature, *Indian Writing in English*. While he has been criticized as being sexist for lumping all Indian women writers in one chapter, we do find that he attributes the beginning of the literature to the daring of Aru and Toru Dutt, who like Sarojini Naidu (they merit their own chapters interestingly), strove to storm the Western publishing empires by sending off their work to critics like Gosse. This set the precedent for the giants of Indian writing in English, like R.K. Narayan, to send their work off to Westerners like Graham Greene. And as Gosse said of the Dutt sisters, "When Poetry is as good as this, it does not matter whether Rouveyer prints it on Whatman paper or whether it steals to light in blurred type from some press in Bhawanipore." (Iyengar 58) Similarly, Gosse encouraged Naidu to explore and narrate "the heart of India" (Iyengar, 209). As feminists we can of course find fault with these proclamations on two grounds: (1) that these are solitary examples standing out among women mostly oppressed; and (2) that they are taking validation from Western men who in turn are encouraging them to "exoticise the East" or in Edward Said's words they were turning these women into Orientalists. And yet we can argue, that despite being tokens, these "subalterns" were actually "speaking." As we recover the history of our own literatures and engage in projects of recovery, we will see that we do not actually need postcolonial theorists or Western theorists to give shape to our articulations. We do not need the concept of "feminism" imported from the West to give a name to the leaderships forged by Indian women. Take simply here a male writer's creation of the character of a woman who is a leader in our "independence resistance." Venkamma in Raja Rao's *Kanthapura* (New Directions, 1963) uses her powers of storytelling of the myths to rouse a whole village's worth of women to resistance.

Indian women have always had "power" and "sisterhood," even under the worst of oppressions, most of these oppressions having come to them from women, mothers-in-law or "other women," as we find in Anita Desai's classic novel, *Voices in the City* (1965), where the oppressive mother-in-law drives Monisha into living self-immolation in a mockery of bride burning, an act that has a profound influence on her younger sister. As we look at how women oppress women, we also see how the male who dominates and destroys is empowered to do so by a sort of authority given by the older woman.

My use of the term "sisterhood" can be criticized for drawing from Western feminism and the relatively young "feminist" movement of the U.S., compared to India, where we have had generations of strong women. While sisterhood has always referred to the connection between sisters and sometimes to the connection among women in religious orders, it was the U.S. feminist Kathie Sarachild who used *sisterhood,* as synonymous with "power," where solidarity among resisting women could break down power structures. It then became the title of Robin Morgan's influential anthology *Sisterhood is Powerful* (Random House, 1970), an emblem of women's liberation and resistance. After some decades of distance from the powerful solidarity of the women's movement, women in the U.S. are again turning to such "sisterhood," as can be seen in the Women's March in Washington, the general "pink" hat resistance to Trump. And again, not to borrow from "The West," but to say that as women in the U.S. and elsewhere are recovering their powers, it is time for us to also engage in what Latin American Studies calls "recovery projects," not just to recover older works (as Daisy Rockwell is doing with her new editions of Kahdija Mastur's work), but to recover forgotten and early texts of Indian women writing in English. In the plethora of burgeoning new Indian/ South Asian writing in English, both from India and "the west," in the rush to create and get on the publishing train, we forget the quiet voices, never seen as feminist and daring, but making the points so relevant today.

One of the earliest texts, which we should read in the era of #MeToo is Kamala Markandaya's *Two Virgins*. A quietly told tale buried in what we could consider insignificant early Indian writing in English, we have a story currently playing out with other players in other countries, across T.V. screens, and internet social media, a story of the (s)exploitation of young girls. Two young ladies, Lalitha and Saroja, living in a small village Chingelput, find themselves the attention of a film producing company that comes to town. Dazzled by the producer and dazzled with the opportunity to become a film star, Lalitha lords it over her sister, "A film star, said Lalitha, a film actress, a personality of the cinema. . . . It was my dancing, said Lalitha. It caught his eye, she took his fancy." (53)

A veritable Harvey Weinstein had invaded this little village, left a little girl to be pregnant and have an abortion, as whoever was Mr. Gupta *ghosted* (to use contemporary vocabulary) the little girl.

> Not girls from families like ours, said Amma. These are low class girls with low intelligence. She was wrong. Lalitha was none of these things, but Lalitha was pregnant. From time to time there had been other girls like her too. Exceptions that proved the rule, claimed Amma. She stuck to her belief, even after Lalitha. But she was less vocal. A family like theirs had produced a girl just like the others. (136)

The blame here is on the victim and it is from another woman. Always, women blaming women, even their own daughters. The story of the exploitation of two sisters is retold, almost intertextually by Rasana Atreya, in her *Tell a Thousand Lies*, (nominated for the Tibor Jones South Asia Prize) where the twins Pullama and Lata are taken advantage of by corrupt politicians.

But what is important in these stories is that there is an actual "sisterhood," sisters who stand by each other, even as older women who should have the power to do so, don't. And it is from that sisterhood that the power comes.

"Sisters" have become a very powerful metaphor in South Asian women's writings, perhaps due to the need for some solidarity with another who is not the oppressor. Monica Ali's *Brick*

*Lane* has parallel interconnected stories of sisters. Two Bangladeshi sisters, Hasina and Nazneen, have two different fates. Hasina remains in Bangladesh while Nazneen is "sent away," as the author says, to London, presumably to marry the puffy faced Chanu. Her life is "foreign" alien and untenable among people she does not know and among whom she is unable to forge sisterhoods, until her own twin girls come along, who are veritably her sisters. The girls, Bibi and Shahnaz, become her "partners in crime," as it were, not really any crime, but the crime of westernization of moving away from the overly Islamicized life style of a liberally educated Chanu, who should be able to make something of his life, but is unable because of the isolation of the immigrant. The poignancy of the isolation that Nazneen feels is rivalled only by the touching descriptions of isolated housewives in New Jersey as described by Jhumpa Lahiri, in the opening story of *The Interpreter of Maladies* (Houghton Mifflin, 1999). In her loneliness, Nazneen forges a relationship with Karim, who brings her sewing to occupy her life. Letters fly back and forth between the sisters, one in Bangladesh and the other in London. Both lives are restricted. And yet, in her isolation, Nazneen is gradually becoming westernized, liberated, learning from her daughters that there is another way of life: "This is England, you can do whatever you like," her daughters teach her. Her liberation comes when both, her husband Chanu and the man she had befriended Karim, leave for Bangladesh to fight the Islamicist cause.

Another type of sisterhood is forged in Zadie Smith's *White Teeth*. A novel written by a Caribbean Black British writer, it looks at South Asian women in the context of the council flats, where Nazneen of *Brick Lane* has been transported. Truly a multicultural novel, it gives South Asian women a choice as it were: "make your connections or forever remain isolated. In this, a new kind of sisterhood emerges, that of making bonds across cultures, as a way of retaining and centring one's power. Alsana the Bangladeshi woman, Clara, the Caribbean, Jehovah's witness and Neena become a little sewing "clatch," like a coffee clatch and in it is their means of survival, in the grit of the council flats, that their lives are relegated to. While technically they have no power, it is in the coming together that they have the strength to survive.

It is often in the depicting of the lives of these women that the younger and newer authors have found their strength and survival, their sisterhood, power and daring. As each of these women characters or authors finds strength to break out from oppression as a result of "sisterhood," whether actual relationship, or a forged connection, we see the strength of South Asian women shine forth, whether in India or overseas.

## Works Cited

Ali, Monica, *Brick Lane*, London: Scribner, 2003

Atreya, Rasana, *Tell a Thousand Lies*, Amazon, 2012

Iyengar, K.R. Srinivasa, *Indian Writing in English,* Bombay: Asia, 1973.

Markandaya, Kamala, *Two Virgins*, NY: Signet, 1973.

Smith, Zadie, *White Teeth*, NY: Vintage, 2001

# Indian Women's Autobiographies: Mosaic of Multiculturism

**S. VENKATA ARUNA**
**Swami Vivekananda Institute of Technology, Secunderabad**

Autobiography as a genre lends an array of insights into not just the influences that shaped the autobiographer's life but importantly into the social landscape of the day. The cultural constructs, in fact, read like a subtext, shaping the author's persona at large so much so that the personal life stands hinged to the social, historical, cultural pegs of the day. Though every autobiographer finds the social influence looming large over his life, it is women autobiographers who provide a wider social space in their writings as their lives are deeply influenced by and interwoven into the social fabric. The autobiographies are a rich repertoire of contemporary history and culture.

Indian women autobiographies bring to the fore, among other things, the multicultural background of India. The autobiographers that the researcher has chosen hail from different parts of India. The narratives brim with the rich cultural diversity that India is home to and present a colourful patina of cultural hues. As Jawaharlal Nehru says, "The diversity of India is tremendous; it is obvious. It lies on the surface and anybody can see it. It concerns itself with physical appearances as well as with certain mental habits and traits. . . . Yet, with all these differences, there is no mistaking the impress of India." (61)

Savitri Devi Nanda from Lahore, Amrita Pritam from Delhi, Nayantara Sahgal from Allahabad, Kamala das from Kerala, Cornelia Sorabjee from Pune, and Durgabai Deshmukh from Rajahmundry, belong to culturally diverse backgrounds and yet as we read these autobiographies, to quote Nehru once again, 'there is no mistaking the impress of India.' (62)

Multiculturism is the existence of different cultures and traditions in a country. According to K.V. Dominic, 'Multiculturalism is defined as the state of co-existence of diverse cultures.'

In India, each state upholds a diverse culture and with different languages and dialects, each region is a separate entity of its own. The multiple groups retaining their cultural niche and respecting other cultures is the hallmark of Indianness. For a country which has been ransacked by invading cultures, and whose economic graph has not been very encouraging due to social and political reasons, it is indeed very surprising that Indian cultural kaleidoscope is able to preserve its harmonious template throughout. Neither the under-development of the country and the illiteracy nor a host of regional differences could stymie the idea of multiculturism. As in the West, muticulturism in India is neither a salad bowl nor a melting pot but a colourful mosaic where integration and independence strike a fine balance and co-exist. Harihar Bhattacharyya gives a vivid account of India's multiculturism

> India is the second most populous country (population now over a billion) after China, and socially and culturally the most diverse in the world. Formed over many thousands of years as a country of immigrants who brought their own cultures and traditions, India's diversity is proverbial. Although predominantly inhabited by "Hindus" (over 82 per cent) who are regionally rooted, plural in beliefs and practices, and divided by castes and languages, India's population also includes a large proportion of Muslims (about 12 per cent), Sikhs, Buddhists, Christians and Jains. Linguistically too, India is very diverse.

Rochana Bajpai elucidates: 'India is an outstanding case for the study of multiculturism.' We find multicultural strands in the writings of Indian women autobiographies as they walk the readers through the female experiences they have undergone in the given cultural context.

Savitri Devi Nanda's autobiography *The City of Two Gates*, Kamala Das's *My Story*, Cornelia Sorabjee's *India Calling*, Amrita Pritam's *Life and Times*, Nayantara Sahgal's *Prison and Chocolate Cake* and *From Fear Set Free* and Durgabai Deshmukh's *Chintaman and I* are poignant self-narratives of women who at the threshold of the twentieth century found a path to hoist their dreams on the pegs of their new-found individuality that education had bestowed upon them. When compared to the earlier women autobiographers of India, the twentieth century women writers chose to express their innermost feelings and social taboos without inhibitions.

In spite of the professional stature they have attained, their narratives brim with the culture of the land they belong to since their lives are interwoven into the cultural fabric. Savitri Devi Nanda, a diffident girl in a wealthy, male-dominated joint family, is fortunate enough to find a sympathetic father who weans her away from the conventional role thrust on women and encourages her to pursue medical course in England. The child marriages, festivities, undue importance given to boys in the family, social bonding during community gatherings, restrictions imposed on girls during their stay in hostels form a backdrop of the narrative.

Kamala Das's account of her life in *My Story* which begins with a humiliation of a brown child in a European school familiarizes the reader to the cultural practices of Kerala in South India. Born to educated parents and into a family of literary eminence, young Kamala describes a host of practices that her Nalapat House is home to. The traditional castor oil rituals, bathing in the rivers, grandmother spinning khadi, the influence of Gandhi streaming down from his portrait hanging on the wall, growing up under the stern gaze of the parents, association with Kamala's great-grandmother and her younger sister, the norms of a matrilineal family introduce the reader to a culture typical to Kerala. The vivid description of Nalapat house with its orchards and snake hills, shrines and servants, forms a backdrop to her narrative and at a later point in the story, the same ancestral house stands as mute witness and sympathizer to her carnal and karmic frustrations. The social life of Kerala forms a vivid contrast to the north Indian culture portrayed in the memoirs of Savitri Devi, Amrita Pritam and Nayantara Sahgal. The autobiographies reveal 'both the cultural economy in which women write and the politics of canon building as it affected women.'

Cornelia Sorabjee, in her *India Calling* had a secure, disciplined childhood under the loving care of her Parsi parents. Growing up among many siblings in the 'patches of dappled sunshine' at Nasik, she has fond recollections of her parental love laced with discipline and owes her cosmopolitan attitude in diet and general upbringing to the Christian, Parsee and Indian influences. She learnt the concept and practice of social service from her mother, who instilled in her daughter the feeling that there is nothing to fear—but fear. Though she had a brilliant academic record and a Barrister degree from Oxford, Cornelia could not register herself as a lady lawyer as there was no precedent. Hence she took up to offer legal counsel to the puradanasheen, the secluded women of the Kathiawar state. Cornelia writes about the rituals and customs of the Purdanasheen homes, the stunted growth of the women and the gradual change that had set in their lives and how they were sent to schools with purdahs and followed the practice of living in veil culture though in its scaled-down version. Her victories in handling the zenana property and in educating the young in handling finances, and her adventures in-between, in the most inhospitable forest and land terrains make for a gripping narrative. In Cornelia Sorabjee's words, 'The opportunity of studying real people of India in their setting; the opportunities of travelling off the beaten track, of learning legend, folklore and custom; best of all, the delight of contact with the Indian purdahnasheen' gave her the utmost satisfaction (132).

Amrita Pritam resurrects the social time as she winds her way from the early memories of her school teacher and parents, her childhood in Western Punjab, the stern discipline of a spiritualist father and the influence of the Sikh guru culture at home. Losing her mother at the young age of 12 made her a loner and she sought company in books. Gifted with exquisite poetic language, she wielded her pen to paint the social customs of the contemporary society. The physical and emotional turbulence that came in the wake of Partition and the social repercussions find a poignant mention in her work. Like Kamala Das, she too gave a fluid expression to her uninhibited emotions in her writings and they created social ripples.

Nayantara Sahgal's twin autobiographies reflect her values and the changing values of society. Born into the illustrious Nehru family, her social narrative is steeped in the political events of India's independence struggle. The social fabric of the day was full of Gandhian aura.

Another firebrand political activist and pioneer of women empowerment from Andhra Pradesh, Durgabai Deshmukh weaves her story from the Gandhian influence of the day in her Kakinada town where she was born. She took up cudgels against the social evils even as a child under the influence of Gandhi and grew up to establish several women empowerment centres. Her life itself is a shining example of the social transformation she chose for herself.

The women autobiographers offer different multicultural insights; when the students get to read these narratives, they get an opportunity to appreciate the multicultural mosaic that India has always been. They are like multicoloured flowers with different fragrances, but they stand in the same garden and exude universal charm.

## Works Cited

Rochana Bajpai, "Multiculturism in India: An Exception?" www.bu.edu/cura

Harihar Bhattacharyya, "Multiculturalism in Contemporary India," *International Journal on Multicultural Societies*, 5: 2, 2003, 148-61.

Kamala Das, *My Story*, Sterling, New Delhi, 1988.

Durgabai Deshmukh, *Chintaman and I*, Allied, New Delhi.

Savitri Devi Nanda, *The City of Two Gateways: The Autobiography of an Indian Girl*, Simson Shand, London, 1954.

K.V. Dominic, *Multicultural Symphony*. New Delhi: Gnosis, 2014.

Jawaharlal Nehru. *The Discovery of India*. Calcutta: Signet Press, 1946.

Amrita Pritam, *Life and Times*, Vikas, New Delhi, 1989.

Nayantara Sahgal, *Prison and Chocolate Cake* and *From Fear Set Free*, WW. Norton, New York.

Cornelia Sorabjee, *India Calling*, Oxford University Press, New Delhi, 2001.

Susie J. Tharu and K Lalita, *Women Writing in India: The Twentieth Century*, Feminist Press, City University of New York, 1993.

# Tracing the Trajectory of Cultural Interface in Diasporic Situation: A Study of Anita Desai, Jhumpa Lahiri, Kiran Desai and M.G. Vassanji

**JAGDISH BATRA**
**O.P. Jindal Global University, Sonepat**

Literature is not only a reflection of life but also reflection on life. Great minds create great literature that appeals to young minds who, acculturated at an impressionable age, become responsible pillars of society later. Such literature gives universal message of oneness of mankind and decries barriers separating one human being from the other. Imaginary boundaries of nation are under attack in postmodern literature. In a similar vein should be treated the other divisions of colour, sex, race created by nature. These may not appear to be as imaginary as the boundaries of man-made caste (specific to India) and religion but one must transcend the concrete and comprehend the ontology of invisible spirit.

Tracing the trajectory of cultural interface in fiction written by writers of Indian stock is an interesting exercise. I have selected four novels belonging to different timeframes and locales. These are: Anita Desai's *Baumgartner's Bombay* which is poignant study of a twice-relocated German Jew in India; Jhumpa Lahiri's *The Namesake* which relates the experiences of an Indian couple and their children born and brought up in the US; Kiran Desai's *The Inheritance of Loss* which places a lower class Indian as an illegal immigrant in the US; and M.G.

Vassanji's *No New Land* in which the people of Indian origin, long resident in Kenya, have to migrate to Canada to start life afresh. These, I suppose, provide multiple perspectives from terrains as remote as Asia, Africa, Europe and America, and spanning a long period of time.

The selection underlines the postmodern condition in which we lead lives today. As an example, let me take the novel *The Inheritance of Loss* with parallel stories of a teenage girl Sai who comes to her grandfather in India after losing her India-born but Russia-resident parents; and a poor Indian cook's son, Biju trying to find employment in USA. There are also native Indians being treated as outsiders by the Gorkha militants fighting for statehood in the area of Darjeeling, where we come across multiple cultures represented by different characters. None of the human beings living in an old building named Cho Oyu are the original inhabitants of this place. Even the building, built by a Scotsman, is now the property of Jemubhai. The neighbours include Uncle Potty, an anglophile from Lucknow and Father Booty, a Swiss national who came here 45 years ago and never thought of going back. Thus, the underlying idea is migrancy which affects most people in the world today and which brings in its trail the multicultural interactions.

There have been many waves of migration from India throughout history, which can broadly be divided into two categories: willing and forced migrations. It would be worthwhile to note that "Even though distinction has to be made between forced and willing movement of people, the phenomenon of diaspora necessarily involves a structure of location followed by dislocation and relocation. Moving away from one's homeland and settling elsewhere on a short-term basis does mean dislocation that brings in a sense of loss and nostalgia. This is followed by a bid for relocation in an alien milieu through negotiation and adjustment. And yet there is no guarantee that the outcome will be sure success; hybridity or in-betweenness being quite common here" (Malik & Batra 153).

For all this talk of multiculturalism, the fact remains that for an immigrant, the ground reality is different in the host society into which he situates himself. The tell-tale colour and features of his face and body, his dress sense and demeanour are enough to assign him an alien's status in a society far removed from his land. In this, Anita Desai's protagonist Baumgartner's plight indeed evokes pathos. "Accepting but not accepted" (20)—that, in short, sums up the story of Hugo Baumgartner. He is an alien in his own land as he was too dark, clearly marked a Jew, out of favour with the Nazis who had freshly come to power. Self-exiled to India, he found he was too fair and that marked him as an outsider, a *firangi.*

In Jhumpa Lahiri's *The Namesake* the protagonist Ashima's accent distinguishes her from others. Her son Gogol's name becomes the subject of fun in his school because the name is neither American, nor Indian but Russian! He finally goes in for change of name when he is studying in college but that turns him into a divided self—an identity crisis at its worst with which most immigrants have to live. When Ashoke returns with his family from India, he is flabbergasted to see the name of the family on letterbox painted over so that 'Gangulis' has become 'Gangreen.' (67)

In Vassanji's *No New Land*, Nurdin Lalani, the young protagonist, a travelling shoe-salesman in East Africa, has to shift to Canada, following the turmoil in his home country in the aftermath of independence and the subsequent nationalist moves which edge out the Indian-origin East Africans. Nurdin migrates to Canada with his wife, Zera, and their two young children, Fatima and Hanif. He has big dreams of settling in a country which is famed as a land of plenty with ample opportunities of individual growth for everyone.

As immigrants, when they land in Canada, they are awestruck by the glitz and glamour and the opulence seen everywhere. The ethnic prejudice is represented in the novel by the attack on Nurdin's neighbour Esmail. He gets caught in mock fighting among three Canadian young men. They taunt him as "Paki," leer and jeer at him, inviting the attention of the people around, but nobody comes to Emsail's rescue and the poor fellow is thrown on to the railway track. He is saved before the train arrives but the wounds take long to heal.

Culture shock is a well-recognized phenomenon that comes into play in such a situation. According to Webster's Dictionary, it is "a state of confusion and uncertainty sometimes with feelings of anxiety that may affect people exposed to an alien culture or environment without adequate preparation." This confusion and uncertainty is experienced most acutely when the ethical sentiments are affected. For example, in *No New Land*, we find that upon arrival in Canada, Nurdin is invited to John McCormack's party. People of different ethnicities have gathered in a large lobby shimmering with chandeliers. A fashion show is organized on the occasion. As the female models walk past on the ramp in their fashionable innerwear and high-heeled shoes, Nurdin overhears the disapproving conversation between Roshan and Zera:

> "This is the kind of thing we have to steer our kids from," said Zera.
>
> "Precisely, sister," said Roshan, "We have something to give to this country. Morals, I say." (55-56)

Back home, Nurdin had been brought up in a strict orthodox Muslim way, but here in Canada, he finds what he refers to as the 'easy' culture: "He had never seen anything like this, not in ads, not in movies, nor even the girlie magazines of his youth. Sex beyond his wildest dreams: dirty depraved exciting—how much the flesh was capable of?" (145). This conflict within him is accentuated in a rather laughable way, for whenever he looks up at the picture of his father hung on the wall, he feels a pull being exerted on him from what his basic instincts would impel him towards. Thus, for the present generation, the old generation, though dead and gone, still evokes awe.

Baumgartner has the shock of his life when he lands in jail in India—something that he had dreaded in Germany. India was under the British yoke and Britain was enemy of Germany in the Second World War So, he is taken to the Central internment camp at Ahmednagar, where the so-called 'hostile aliens' from all over India were imprisoned. They are all screened to find out the reasons and Baumgartner appears before the officer to convince him that he is a harmless person. But even after appearing in more than one interviews and spending hours standing in slow-moving queues, all his arguments are shoved off with a smirk: "Got a German passport, says you were born there—then what am I supposed to take you for, a bloomin' Indian?" The papers were flung at him, and he retreated, baffled, wondering what magic world he might find that would release him from what was a monstrous mistake, or madness. (106)

Baumgartner has another shock when his identity is fixed by the street urchins: "pagal sahib, billi wallah sahib" (204) which means "he is crazy man—the man with the cats." That is because he takes to tending to stray cats, out of the lesson of piety and sympathy that he has learnt through his own rejection by his countrymen as also by the people of his adopted land, i.e., India. His condition is indeed pathetic; surely the maladjustment can even lead to "medical condition" with symptoms like "a feeling of helplessness and a desire for dependence on long-term residents of one's own nationality; . . . finally, that terrible longing to be back home" (Oberg 143).

Even though much voluntary migration takes place out of desire to improve the economic lot, there is no guarantee that it will lead of overnight transformation. It is truer in case of forced migration. Baumgartner, as a child, had seen in Hitler's Germany his father being taken away, his business being taken over by a non-Jew, his mother trying somehow to manage the family, his own forced migration to India in search of a better life. But here in India, under British rule, he is taken to be a German spy at one time. When he is released from the camp, his business is found to have been taken over by his partner's son who refuses to have anything to do with Baumgartner. He wondered:

> if the long internment had not incapacitated him, made him unfit for the outer world. And what would they find outside? Germany destroyed—no possibility of returning, so that he would have to accept India as his permanent residence. He wondered at his ability to survive in it, reduced as he was to such an abject state of helplessness, and the knowledge of being alone. (133)

In *The Inheritance of Loss*, we find that the teenager girl Sai's parents had also gone to Russia to earn livelihood, but unfortunately they met with a fatal accident. That is why Sai, who had been studying in a convent, had to come to her only surviving relative—Jemubhai. This story is pitted against the story of the cook's son Biju. Trying to settle in far-off America, Biju is moving from one ill-paid job to the other and also, while working in stuffy kitchens, coming in contact with people from other third world countries—from Pakistan to Zanjibar. Racial prejudices present hurdles in earning livelihood in the world even in post-modern times. In America, the conditions of work for illegal immigrants are not sound. They live in constant fear of being spotted by the police and are exploited by cheats on the pretext of helping them to get green card.

In the severe New York winter, Biju has to put a padding of newspaper under his shirt to keep himself warm. From Baby Bistro to Brigette's, Biju woks in many restaurants before he is finally rendered jobless. The owners of the Brigette's restaurant are shown aware of the machinations of the powerful in the world to dominate their home country's politics and economy through economic imperialism. People like Achootan want green card as a matter of right with the logic which he had developed in England: "Your father came to *my* country and took *my* bread and now I have come to *your* country to get *my* bread back" (135). This is raw logic but surely it has a lot of sense in it.

In *No New Land*, we find that the living quarters at Sixty-nine Rosecliff Park Drive bring home the reality of the immigrants. Compulsions of survival have trained them to turn the residential quarters into business ones. Nurdin has problems adjusting in the adopted land. It is not only the new culture, but also the strain of finding a proper job. He is looked upon as an outsider and is not easily believed when he pleads innocence in the case of alleged molestation of a white woman at the workplace.

In these circumstances, the homesickness or nostalgia for the lost homeland is bound to develop. The novel *The Namesake* opens on a nostalgic note. Ashima, newly married to Ashoke and brought to US immediately thereafter, finds the new land lonely and strange. She is admitted to hospital for delivery of baby and even though there are two other women in the ward, waiting to undergo child-birth, Ashima feels lonely and remembers her kinsfolk back in Calcutta. It is traumatizing for her to deliver her first baby away from her relatives who would throng the hospital, if she were in India.

While jobless, Nurdin in *No New Land* finds himself unable to afford a hamburger, and then he grows nostalgic about his Dar-es-Salaam: "On these hopeless trips, how many time you've sniffed the air outside a restaurant, wishing you could afford a hamburger, a hotdog. French fries, but the price of a hamburger here, could buy four in Dominion. Sweaty, tired, and desperate, a state you have never known in Dar" (45).

The young generation that has moved out of India to countries like America, has the old parents back in India. Due to strong family ties, both sides feel the absence of each other.

When a close relative or one of the parents of the expatriate passes away and he or she is not able to fly back to India to be with the other members of the bereaved family, a feeling of remorse overtakes the immigrant. This is what we find in case of Ashoke (*The Namesake*) who goes to India, along with his wife and children, upon getting news of the death of Ashima's father. He spends close to eight months in India, but does not mind it since he enjoys being in India after a long time.

Salman Rushdie's non-fictional book, aptly titled *Imaginary Homelands*, begins with reference to the compulsion of the immigrant to create imaginary homelands. A writer, in his condition, says he, is haunted by "some sense of loss, some urge to reclaim, to look back," but looking back is with the knowledge that "our physical alienation from India almost inevitably means that we will not be capable of reclaiming precisely the thing that was lost, that we will, in short, create fictions, not actual cities or villages, but invisible imaginary homelands, Indias of the mind" (10).

So, wherever the diasporic people are, they try to create their imaginary homelands and the foods and flavours are the essential objects, apart from locations, linked to one's memory. The immigrants in Canada have all sorts of meals of "*chapatis* and rice, meat curries cooked the Goan, Madrasi, Hyderabadi, Gujarati and Punjabi ways, *channa* the Caribbean way, *fou-fou* the West African way" (Vassanji 65).

Sometimes, the effort to create homeland in the adopted land creates misunderstanding. The memory of their native Dar impels some residents to scatter grains for hens which is misinterpreted by the Canadian media as voodoo:

> Several men had complained of waking up some mornings with a heart heavy with nostalgic yearnings and a clear memory of a Dar backyard strewn with grains and busy with the frantic clucking of hens. Why the persistence of that memory, so sharp and clear, over many others? This became clear when a local tabloid arrived one

> morning with the sensational headline: VOODO IN DON MILLS! (61)

But indeed, company of compatriots brings the much-needed solace to the migrants. In *Baumgartner's Bombay*, we find Baumgartner, a jobless wanderer, being comforted by Lotte, a bar dancer of German origin. In *The Namesake*, for example, the writer mentions the special classes which are organized by the Indian community residing in America for the benefit of their children. They celebrate religious and cultural festivals like Diwali, Mundan and marriage collectively so that the children get a feel of their native culture. Ashima takes lead in arranging marriage *a la* Indian style for her son Gogol after his break-up with Maxine.

There is attempt to create the imaginary homeland for the next generation too. As the child grows up, his acculturation becomes a matter of concern to his parents. The Bengali community in America tries to educate their children. Ashima teaches Gogol Tagore's poems, names of deities and festivals etc. He is groomed to call Maya Nandi as Maya Mashi. In the Bengali class arranged by the expatriate Bengali community, Gogol is taught to read and write the alphabet used by his ancestors. Being the son of Indian parents, Gogol is not supposed to take to American values. It is a matter of satisfaction for his parents that "Gogol does not date anyone in high school. . . . He does not attend dances or parties" (93). All that, however, goes out of the window when Gogol comes into his own!

While the immigrants create imaginary homelands in their own ways, it is the attempt at adjustment with the host milieu that can make the diasporic happy. Unless one is willing to make compromises with the host society, one cannot hope to be at peace with oneself or with the world around. In *The Namesake*, Ashoke and Ashima get slowly initiated into American lifestyle:

> Their garage, like every other, contains shovels and pruning shears and a sled. They purchase a barbecue for *tandoori* on the porch in summer. . . . They learn to roast turkeys, albeit rubbed with garlic and cumin and cayenne, at Thanksgiving, to nail a wreath to their door in December, to wrap woolen scarves around snowmen, to color boiled eggs violet and pink at Easter and hide them around the house. For the sake of Gogol and Sonia they celebrate, with progressively increasing fanfare, the birth of Christ, an event the children look forward to far more than the worship of Durga and Saraswati. (64; my italics)

In the process, the diasporic also discover newer, finer aspects of life in alien society. Ashima learns about some good aspects of American society too, as for example, the honesty of the Americans. Her landlord's family is all help when she comes from hospital with her first baby.

But the adjustment is hardly ever perfect. There are instances of in-betweenness, as Ashoke and Ashima cope with their son's dating with the American girl Maxine, even as the relationship ends prematurely because Maxine is not able to appreciate Gogol's longish mourning for his deceased father. Towards the end of the novel, we find a widowed Ashima deciding to spend six months in India and the other six months in the U.S.—a symbolic reconciliatory gesture towards the diasporic's plight.

We find Baumgartner wishing the street watchman in Calcutta: 'Good morning, Salaam,' and going down the steps into the street with his bag, uncertain as ever of which language to employ. After fifty years, still uncertain, Baumgartner Du Dummkopf" (13). Communication is hostage to culture and Baumgartner has yet to learn a lot, after 50 years!

This is in line with what Homi Bhaba opines with regard to hybridity. In any process of acculturation, the possibility of change exists at all moments of life, so we get hybrid characters rather than pure subjectivities: "The social articulation of difference, from the minority perspective, is a complex, on-going negotiation that seeks to authorize cultural hybridities that emerge in moments of historical transformation" (2).

There are various levels of adjustment reached—starting from maladjustment to integration to assimilation, but none of these is totally compartmentalized experience. A comparison is drawn in the novel *No New Land* between the families of Nurdin and his niece Nermine, daughter of his brother, who came earlier to Canada. She has adopted the Western lifestyle and presents the picture of a partially assimilated Asian immigrant. There are others like Nurdin who live between two worlds, neither of which can be their permanent bulwark. The occupants of Sixty-nine Rosecliff Park Drive "assert their 'Indianness' and 'Africanness' by living their own private lives and they perceive this as a way of maintaining their identity in an environment which would otherwise provide little satisfaction" (Mridula 134).

The adjustment requires the spirit of give and take. Romesh also tries to wean Nurdin away from traditional path. He brings him round to eat pork and drink beer and even takes him to a peep-show. Nurdin is a conscientious fellow who scrutinizes his own self for his deviance from the straight path. But his children, particularly the daughter Fatima, do not toe the traditional path. She is steeped in Canadian culture and hates the African connection: "She was ashamed of this little Paki-shitty-stan of Don Mills, as she called it. She didn't belong here" (167).

In *No New Land*, a solution to resolve the inter-culture differences is suggested by Jamal's father, who edited a magazine *Atom*. He favoured cohabitation and marriages between people of different cultures! (72). Quite an effective solution, but he did not find favour with authorities and was dismissed from job! What the novelist suggests is that revolutionary methods are not easily accepted by a traditional society.

When the British rulers took away farm workers as "indentured labour" from India to work in the sugarcane fields of colonies as far away as Fiji, Guyana, Surinam, etc., the workers developed fellow feeling on the ships and the term *jahaz bhai* or "brothers of ships" was coined to symbolize this relationship. Working far away from homeland and with no hope of ever returning because they were paid subsistence wages only, this fellow feeling sustained them. In the novel *No New Land*, it is the residue of that "jahaz bhai" spirit seen in the support by fellow East Africans that makes life easier for the immigrants. When Mohan from Guyana is stuck up with his wife at Sixty-nine Apartment Block, Nurdin provides them shelter. Next day, when Mohan's brother Romesh reaches Nurdin's house to take his brother away, he gets introduced to Nurdin and this introduction is instrumental in getting Nurdin a job. The attack on Esmail brings back memories of such events back in Dar for many immigrants. But one thing that comes out clear is the support of the fellow immigrants who continue to visit his home to ask after his health. However, not everywhere do we have the picture of unity among immigrants. Kiran Desai examines the exploitation of Indians by Indians in America. Harish Harry is a perfect businessman who won't travel the extra mile to help his compatriots. Do the exploiters forget their common home?

The individual immigrant is thus faced with a number of difficulties and has willy-nilly to make adjustments. It is not only the alien milieu, but also the politics of the adopted country that has a bearing on the life of the immigrant and his family. Politics is the name of the power game. So, politicians anywhere would see which way their bread is buttered and accordingly support or oppose the cause of the migrant. Who would know better about it than the European people who are pitted against the influx of refugees running away from IS? In democratic India, the term 'vote bank' denotes the dominant tendency of the political class to decide on issues such as the influx of Bangladeshi refugees into India. A piquant situation is created when the politicians eye the sizeable Bangladeshi votes in Assam and other north-eastern states while the native people oppose encroachment on their land

and resources. The jobs are grabbed in a cut-throat competition by the starving immigrant as the local people experience heart burning. This scenario is depicted by Suravi Sarma Kumar in her novel *Voices in the Valley* (2012).

An opposite picture is presented in the novel *The Inheritance of Loss*. We find that the local Gorkha activists flex their muscles and encroach upon land duly purchased by outsiders, as a pressure tactic to demand statehood for their region from the Indian government. Again, politicians stand to gain from this scenario rather than the ordinary people.

In *No New Land*, we find that in the aftermath of the attack on Esmail and the solidarity shown by the fellow Asians towards him, the local left political parties organize a rally to support Esmail's cause. In any case, the point which I seek to highlight is that politics is a ubiquitous phenomenon and the diasporic population too senses it. Bhikhu Parekh, while examining J. Raz's ethical stance on politics, views the equation between two cultures as a set of competing ones instead of being an ethical one:

> Cultures do not coexist peacefully. They compete, come into conflict and struggle for domination and mastery. Since they are rarely equal numerically or in their political and economic power, moral and political status, and so on, the dominant culture has built-in advantages and tends over time to overwhelm the rest. (97)

This indeed is the ground reality, but at the same time we find that the need for a sound relationship between different communities has become vital in today's globalized world. It is for this reason that different approaches like 'melting pot,' 'cultural mosaic,' etc. have been tried in USA, Canada, UK, Australia, etc. With the rise in global terrorism, even the liberal democratic societies have started calling for assimilation rather than integration. The question is how to bring about a happy integration where both sides interact to mutual advantage.

The imperatives of economic competition, social interaction and political machination make the interface quite complex and intricate. In today's world, multiculturalism is a reality that has to be accepted. Identity politics, if taken too far, lapses into jingoistic assertion on the part of the dominant community. At the same time, the minority community too has a duty to build bridges with the majority community.

These bridges cannot be built merely on the basis of economic benefit. Liberal democracies have implemented laws, introduced learning courses in educational institutions and organized events to bring about better understanding of diasporic communities. Humanity has pinned hope on art and literature and it is the duty of all related to these genres to rise above political ideologies and work for harmony. The rise of terrorism inspired by religious fundamentalism has put a big spanner in the wheel of multiculturalism. It is time we examined critically and impartially rather than subserviently the tenets of religions laid down centuries ago. Rather than any organized religion with its symbolism and ritualism, we need to discover principles of true spirituality which locates universal brotherhood on the basis of spirit and not body. Such spirituality will pave the way for feeling of peaceful co-existence and non-violence and that is what we need the most in today's world.

## Works Cited

Bhabha, H. 1994. *The Location of Culture*. London & New York: Routledge.

Desai, A. 2007. *Baumgartner's Bombay*. New Delhi: Random House.

Desai, Kiran. 2006. *The Inheritance of Loss: A Novel*. New Delhi: Penguin.

Kumar, S.S. 2012. *Voices in the Valley*. New Delhi: Rupa.

Lahiri, Jhumpa. 2003. *The Namesake*. New Delhi: Harper Collins.

Malik, R.S. & J. Batra. 2014. *A New Approach to Literary Theory & Criticism*. New Delhi: Atlantic.

Mridula K.T. & B. Gaonkar. 2015. "Assimilation and Diasporic Sensibility in M.G. Vassanji's *No New Land*," *The Commonwealth Review*, 24 (1): 130-37.

Oberg, K. 1960; 2006. "Cultural Shock: Adjustment to New Cultural Environments," *Practical Anthropology*. New York: Technical Information Clearing House 7: 177-82.

Parekh, B. 2006. *Rethinking Multiculturalism: Cultural Diversity and Political Theory*. New York: Palgrave Macmillan.

Rushdie, Salman. 1992. *Imaginary Homelands*. London: Granta.

Vassanji, M.G. 1991; 1997. *No New Land*. Toronto: McClelland & Stewart.

# Existential Agony of a Woman in Anita Desai's *Voices in the City*

**SANGOJU RAJESWARI**
**Language Expert, DCEB Assessment Cell, SCERT, Nellore**

Anita Desai emphasizes a whole range of themes like man's sense of alienation, in what has come to be termed as "The psychological novel," which also presents a clear contrast to the earlier modes of simple narrative techniques.

In her novel *Voices in City* (1965), Anita Desai is not concerned with the physical aspect of the city, Calcutta, but with its influence on the three characters of family. The novel is divided into four sections, namely, 'Nirode,' 'Monisha,' 'Amla' and 'Mother.' The first section 'Nirode' is about the alienation and conflict in the mind of Nirode. He is an artist who is struggling with art form and his life. He brings out a magazine *Voice* but is not happy with its success and ultimately sells it. He is a person who loves anonymity and runs away from success and prosperity. Nirode also suffers from Oedipus complex, like Maya; and like her, he wants to destroy the figure of his obsession, his mother. He believes that his mother has an affair with Major Chadha, her neighbour. He wants to forget this episode and so alienates himself from his mother. The novelist has probed into the psychic working of the disturbed artist who has lost his faith in life. Madhusudan Prasad writes: "Desai delves deep into human psyche and tries to explore very adroitly the dim domains of the conscious of the major characters in this novel."

Monisha, like many heroines of Anita Desai, is sensitive and suffers from an ill-matched marriage. She lacks understanding and love from her husband, and finds it difficult to adjust into the joint family. She takes to diary writing and alienates herself from everyone. She is an example of maladjusted woman who is an introvert. Monisha is unable to bear the charge of theft by the family members and commits suicide by self-immolation. Amla, her youngest sister, a commercial artist, too suffers from conflict in her life. She rises above the complexities of relationships to realize the destroyer. She is described as an onlooker, not getting involved with the affairs of her children.

In this novel one sees faulty adjustment in the marriage of Mr. and Mrs. Ray, the father and the mother. It was a marriage of convenience, the husband priding himself in his family name and title, and wife on her tea-estates and a house. Both of them have a soul-destroying hatred towards each other. The father transforms into a drunkard, debased, and dishonourable creature; whereas the mother changes into a practical, possessive woman, losing all her womanly charm and warmth.

She is polished and balanced, yet very cold, with a frosty love of power, like a concealed fluorescent bulb. Their marriage was something of a financial settlement. Amla, the daughter, says to Dharma about her father whether he regretted it later on because "he hadn't quite bargained for mother, just for her houses and tea-estates."

The father did nothing except sleeping, drinking and idling. The only thing he did with his sons was to train them to play cricket and he loved horses. "He was always drinking and smiling, his knowing, spiteful smile, with an emotion in him that must have been very violent to show at all in his face, even so faintly."

There was hardly any common liking among the couple. The mother loved music, nature and all the fine things of life: "My father always got on her nerves by simply never doing anything.

I always see him lying back indolently, like an overfed house cat, against mother's embroidered Tibetan cushions, toying with a cheroot or a glass of whisky or both." The musical soirees arranged by her were of no interest to the husband. The sweet music would affect all the guests and even the children, but the husband would remain immune to it. He lay against a bolster, smiling a vacant, feline smile and drinking; and with the passing of hours he fell asleep—his head drooping forward and his mouth open and wet. The sweet '*shehnai*' was no better than a noisy pipe, a piece of plumbing to him. Wife, too, had contempt and resentment for him. Husband had the same hatred and malice towards her: "When he came to Kalimpong and saw her wandering about her garden, touching her flowers, he never followed her. He used to lie back against his cushions, idle and contended—contended I think, in his malice."

He had contempt for his wife's love for nature. He used to taunt and make fun of her when he tells his daughters to look at a butterfly and 'Forget yourself in that study. Then you will be fortunate—like your mother.' The truth was that the wife had deliberately forgotten him; shut her mind to him by concentrating on flowers and music and fine food, and things he shunned. This hatred between the father and mother leaves a scar on the mind of the children. They are the real sufferers.

Monisha, the elder daughter, is childless and is a victim of an ill-matched marriage. Jiban and Monisha had nothing in common between them and were married because he belonged to a respectable, middle-class Congress family which was safe, secure and sound. Her father thought: "Monisha ought not to be encouraged in her morbid inclinations and that it would be a good thing for her to be settled into such a solid, unimaginative family as that, just sufficiently educated to accept her with tolerance."

Monisha changes after marriage from a sensitive, mild, quiet, sensible girl into a barren, distant, without any compassion, neurotic, diary writing woman, which she herself hates. She is happy neither with her husband nor with his family members. Monisha's ill-matched marriage, her loneliness, sterility and stress of living in a joint family with an insensitive husband push her to a breaking point: "My duties of serving fresh chapatis to the uncles as they eat, of listening to my mother-in-law as she tells me the remarkably many ways of cooking fish, of being Jiban's wife."

Jiban is present at home but 'Jiban is never with us at all.' Monisha feels trapped in Calcutta and in the house with the thick iron bars: "I am so tired of it, this crowd. In Calcutta it is everywhere. Deceptively, it is a quiet crowd—passive, but distressed. Till there is reason for anger and then a sullen yellow flame of bitterness and sarcasm starts up and it is vicious and mordant. . . . This boil erupts, every now and then, now that the weather is so hot, the heart so parched."

This view of the city expressed by Monisha shows that she has a loveless life and is misunderstood by everyone. She feels like the bleeding heart doves: "wounded and bleeding, but scurrying about their cages, picking up grain, these stay on the ground, restless, in flux and bleeding."

She faces the trauma of living in a joint family, where there is no private life. She wishes to do work in privacy, away from the aunts and uncles, the cousins and nieces and nephews. She has no privacy even in her own room. It was first regarded as bridal room, but now no longer, as her fallopian tubes were blocked. "The sister-in-law lies across the four-poster, discussing my ovaries and theirs." They make fun of her, as in her wardrobe, instead of saris, there are books. Monisha is the intellectual type who carries her personal library to her in-laws' house. However, nobody bothers about the books she has in her library. Anita Desai has presented the picture of women as daughters-in-law in typical middle class Indian families who are not at all happy. They are reduced to be mere housewives and can do nothing beyond mundane household chores. Jiban tells Monisha, 'Be a little friendly to them. That is all they ask of you—a little friendliness.'

Amla feels sorry for Monisha and wonders how and why it was that she had been married to 'this boring non-entity, this blind moralist, this complacent quoter of Edmund Burke and Wordsworth, Mahatma Gandhi and Tagore, this rotund, minute-minded and limited official.' Jiban was dull and prolix. He worked in a dull Ministry and he would go on talking about his work.

Monisha is accused of theft by everyone in the family. She had taken Jiban's money to pay the hospital bills for Nirode. She had to suffer the humiliation from men and women who are mean and low. The mother-in-law shouts, 'the servants will be dismissed, all of them. I will not have a thief in my house. . . . After all, you were the only person who was in the room all day.' Monisha 'is willing to accept this status then and to live here a little beyond and below everyone else, in exile.' But she is not able to bear this for long and commits suicide by self-immolation. The maladjustment is menacing by the adverse attitude of the family members and hostile social traditions and background.

The other marriages referred to in the novel are also not happy and satisfactory. Dharma, the painter, bears his marriage as it has become his habit. He expresses his idea of marriage to Amla: "Our relationship in not all so straight-forward and pat, married relationship never are. There is the matter of loyalty, habit, complicity . . . things I couldn't talk to you about till you married and knew for yourself."

Dharma and Gita are like strangers. Their daughter had married her cousin, who lived with them for fifteen years. They leave Calcutta and come to live in the suburb, where nobody knew of this incident. Amla feels that Dharma has committed a terrible sin of casting out a young daughter. He says, 'nothing that concerns my daughter concerns me.' His wife prays the whole day, isolating herself even from her husband as if she was repenting in the bubbling prayer of a sinner in despair.

Amla, who was attracted towards Dharma in the beginning, now feels revolted on seeing his other part. She had willingly let herself be lured toward him. The glamour of mystery, his uncanniness, the eeriness about him had lured young girls to his studio. Amla had changed after meeting Dharma. She had grown pale and worked very poorly in the office. She faces swings in her mood; after going to Dharma's house, she would become another Amla, "a flowering Amla, translucent with joy and overflowing with a sense of love and reward." She would like to hear the details. It was only during these hours she felt she was alive. She wanted tangibility and permanence in the relationship which she could not receive from Dharma: "The understanding between them was an interior volcano, colouring the water of his existence and splashing on to his canvas the tints of the upheaval within him."

At times, Amla wondered whether Dharma saw in his model anything more than inspiration which offered him rescue from the complexities of nature in which he had enslaved himself. Amla gets no peace from this relationship. Her aunt, too, advises her to leave him as 'he uses you, something in you that he needs. But the rest—what does he care for that?' At last Amla breaks away from Dharma. She realizes that Gita Devi was the base of all Dharma's actions, 'the spread lotus that bore the weight of the god absorbed in his meditation and the spinning out of his Karma.' Nirode, too, has no faith in man-woman relationship. He is repulsed to see the pretences and show between Jit and Sarla. This couple belongs to the upper class of society. They have no love for each other but live together as it has become a status symbol. Jit is aware of the many admirers of his wife but doesn't say a word about it. Sarla doesn't want to go and meet her in-laws back in south. Nirode feels revulsion for this relationship: "Marriage, bodies, touch and torture ... he shuddered and, walking swiftly, was afraid of the dark of Calcutta. All that was Jit's and Sarla's, he decided, and indeed, all that had to do with marriage, was destructive, negative, decadent."

All the characters in this novel have distrust in marriage. Aunt Lila hates men—particularly her fat, self-centered, long-dead husband. Her opinion is that "women place themselves in bondage to men, whether in marriage or out. All the joy and ambition is channelled that way, while they go parched themselves." She learnt it the hard way. Her daughter, Rita, is also a victim of maladjustment in marriage. She is divorced and working with some of the finest physicists in Paris. Thus, in all the men women relationships mentioned in the novel, we see a picture of desolation and emptiness. They illustrate that marriage, at best, is a farce, at worst, it is a malignancy that destroys body, mind, and soul completely.

## Works Cited

Desai, Anita. *Voices in the City*, Delhi: Orient Paperbacks, 1965.

Srivastava, Ramesh K., ed. "Desai's Theory and Practice of the Novels," *Perspectives on Anita Desai*. Delhi: Vimal, 1984.

Bande, Usha. *The Novels of Anita Desai*, New Delhi: Prestige, 1988.

_____. "Amla-Dharma Love: *Voices in the City*," *Indian Women Novelists*, ed. R.K. Dhawan, vol. 3, New Delhi: Prestige, 1991.

# Partition and Exploitation of Women: A Study of Amrita Pritam's *Pinjar*

**PADMASHREE G.**
**Government First Grade College, Chikkanayakanahalli**

Partition is subjective in literature. Literature being a mirror of society reflects the realistic conditions of the contemporary period and partition of India into India and Pakistan. It was the most far-reaching tragic event in South Asian history which was delineated in various literatures. Many narrations try to look into the effect of traumatic incidents on men, women, communities, society and humanity as a whole.

Partition literature is a multiple combination of historical painful memories of extraordinary human beings. It is a fabric of secularism in the face of communalism. Almost all the novels cover a span of time starting from the days of Partition and deal with partition trauma. The writers also talk about the independence of India and Pakistan followed by massacre, rape, dacoit, loot, fire, mishaps, and many issues related to sufferings of partition.

Amrita Pritam migrated to India during Partition. In Delhi, she lived independently. In that period, she faced many problems. She depicts her women's experiences of the partition. *Pinjar* is a short novel written in 1950 by Amrita Pritam. Originally written in Punjabi, it was translated by Khushwant Singh into English in 2009. The novel depicts the conditions and nature of the Indian society during the partition. Amrita Pritam has poured her own experiences into the novel. She beautifully portrays the women's life during the period of partition. The novel is told from Puro's viewpoint and is a unique glance at Indian partition.

*Pinjar* portrays harrowing situation of women. It is a tale of human mistakes which exploit man's misfortune. A number of cases happen during partition where girls committed suicide without their fault. There are brutal conflicts between families, communities and nations. The novel describes the dominating nature of the males during that period and how women were bound to accept the decisions.

The novel uses historical elements to set off a fictional tale that effectively demonstrates victim's reality. In the beginning, Puro's family is a happy family of two sisters and a brother. Puro is an obedient and ideal daughter. She unquestioningly accepts her parents' decision about her marriage. She starts dreaming about her future with Ramchand, her suitor. The turning point in the story is when Puro is abducted by Rashid, a Muslim boy, who is forced to do this, to avenge a similar act committed by Puro's uncle. Puro tried to free herself but could not get out of his embrace. This portrays how conflicts between families, communities and nation are so often brutally and mindlessly played out on the bodies and identities of women. Rashid does not rape Puro; he keeps her as a prisoner. After struggling a lot she manages to escape and run towards home. She reaches the village and finally the courtyard of her parents' house. But her father tells her that there is no place for her in the family as she had been abducted and her chastity is put to question. Rejection from her own family to accept her is another form of violence she goes through.

Puro is devastated and returns to Rashid to lead a life which is akin to that of a skeleton (Pinjar). Puro's identity undergoes a drastic change. Rashid forces her for marriage and changes her name to Hamida. She now has a new identity which she resists as she longs for her family and marriage to Ramchand. On the other hand Rashid is repentant for the crime of Puro's abduction and seeks redemption. He tries to provide love and care to Puro, but Puro is unrelenting as the wounds inflicted by Rashid are unforgivable. Puro as Hamida comes in contact with three females who were also victims of gender violence. All the three characters are treated merely as body, not as humans. Taro is suffering with some unknown disease and is disowned by her husband. Her husband has brought another woman to live with him and forces Taro to become a prostitute. Her illness and her husband's attitude towards her are unbearable; she wants death to free her from the cage of life. She says to Puro, "What can I tell you, when a girl is given away in marriage, God deprives her of her tongue, so that she may not complain. For full two years, I had to sell my body . . . . I am like a whore, a prostitute . . . there is no justice in the world, nor any God. He [her husband] can do what he likes. There is no God to stop him. God's fetters were only for my feet" (36-38). Amrita Pritam highlights that women are considered nothing more than bodies and violation of women's bodies becomes the moral perversion of the community itself.

Puro meets Kammo, a motherless young girl, who is disowned by her father and stays at her aunt's house. Kammo is ill-treated and exploited by her aunt. Kammo sees Hamida as her mother figure but her aunt stops her to meet Hamida as Hamida is Muslim. Hamida (Puro) realizes that the ultimate victims in all clashes are women, "It was a sin to be alive in this world full of evil, thought Hamida. It was crime to be born a woman" (65).

Hamida used to see a mad woman in her street who was sexually assaulted and was pregnant. The woman was not even aware of the violence inflicted on her body and a child growing in her. She is a victim of a heartless monster of a man. This incident arouses Hamida's pity. When a Muslim woman Hamida decides to take care of a Hindu child, she faces hatred of Hindus. Here the author draws the picture of communal hatred between

Hindus and Muslims. She shows the narrow mind-set of Indian society which is not interested in the child.

The novel depicts the picture of homeless during partition when millions of families were displaced. Innumerable women were kidnapped and raped. The novel also shows that communal hatred was deep-rooted in the minds of Hindus and Muslims. Puro comes to know that few girls from the refugee camp were kidnapped. Lajo, Ramchand's sister, is abducted by a Muslim boy. Ramchand comes to Puro seeking her help. Puro convinces Rashid to help Lajo return back to her home. Puro depicts immense strength in the hour of crisis to help Lajo to escape from the clutches of her abductors. Hamida get an idea of Lajo's new look. She realizes that Lajo had become a victim of gang rape. When Hamida wants to press Lajo's feet, she stops her and says: "Don't touch me! I am unclean! Don't you see, I am a slut, a whore, a common tart?"(43)

Hamida hands Lajo over to Ramchand in the refugee camp. The refugee camp is full of Hindus and Muslims. Those who found themselves an institution similar to Puro and Lajo were finally allowed to leave the camp. In the refugee camp Puro meets her brother Trilok. She comes to know that Ramchand had married her younger sister. Trilok expected Puro to leave her husband and son and return home. Puro became surprised to hear Trilok's words. She feels that she belongs to Rashid.

*Pinjar* is a loaded comment on the threat that communalism posed for women during the days of the post-Partition riots. *Pinjar* represents the social abuse during 1947. Almost all the female characters in the novel are victims of one or the other type of violence. They are oppressed by double yoke of patriarchy and dislocation. As Archana Sinha puts it, "It has been quite disturbing experience all over the world that any conflict, a war, civil strife, communal riots or disturbance women and children became the prime victims of violence. Children are orphaned and women are not only widowed but also become victim of rape and abduction" (43)

## Bibliography

Hiremath, Rudramma, S. "Exposal of false religious dogmatic in *Pinjar*: A Critique," *Literary Cognizance*, I-3 (Dec. 2015): 45-48.

Pritam, Amrita. (2009), *Pinjar*: New Delhi: Tara Press.

Pritam, Amrita. (2003), *The Skeleton and Other Writings*, trans. Khushwant Singh. Mumbai: Jaico.

Sinha, Dr Archana. "Conceptual Study of Violence against Women-The Sociological Dimension," *Women and Violence*. New Delhi: Radha Krishna, 1978.

# The Theme of Expatriation in Bharati Mukherjee's *The Tiger's Daughter*

**FARAHAT NAZNEEN**
**Govt. Degree College, Hyderabad**

Expatriation has existed from the time when there were countries for people to expatriate from. People have always moved about the earth, sometimes making seemingly incredible journeys; empires sent emissaries to other lands, and religious history is full of stories of monks sent to preach religious laws to other countries and missionaries sent by the church to achieve their objectives. Although the term 'expatriate' was used first in the 17th century, often to refer to the 'pioneers' (including artists, authors and entertainers) who left one (usually European) country to make a life elsewhere without any real possibility of return, or to those who renounced their allegiance or were exiled and denaturalized, it was used as a synonym for what we now call 'migrants.'

Globalization has led to increasing international mobility amongst business and education professionals. Drawing on a qualitative study of academics, this paper evaluates the use of metaphor for understanding the "motivation to go" overseas and the "experience" of expatriation. The expatriate include llifestyle migrants that move abroad in search of a better way of life, economic migrants, people that move abroad for economic reasons as they can earn significantly more money and/or have an improved standard of living. The number of people moving country is increasing across all expatriate categories, irrespective of motivation, geographic origin and social background.

The issues raised by the history of English literary expatriation must begin with the question of how closely writers can be associated with their country's cultural experience. Some literature seems indelibly linked to its national origin and some literature seems absolutely untethered to national roots. Generally, expatriate literature deals with alienation, displacement, existential rootlessness, nostalgia and quest of identity. It also addresses issues related to amalgamation or disintegration of cultures. It reflects the immigrant experience that comes out of the immigrant settlement.

Under these circumstances the expatriate sentiments arise in literature. The broken psyche of the expatriates sheds off its impaired emotions into writing. That is how the expatriate writer feels a forceful need to write. They have been successful in transforming their experiences into writings, with their multicultural ethos and a profound understanding of socio-cultural and economic realities around them. Another important reason for writing by the creative talent in the expatriate community is to make their existence recognized. The very act of creation is a purposeful effort to form a cultural identity.

Many women writers of Indian descent have explored the theme of expatriation in their works. India, as the country progressing from tradition to modernity, produced many women writers, who are playing an important role in this transitional period as a harbinger of change. A major segment of the contemporary Indian literature contains fiction produced by women writers. Bharati Mukherjee is one of the prolific writers who got an awareness because of her wide acquaintance with the nuances of life in the East as well as the West. All her major works have enjoyed immense academic attention across the globe and produced a great amount of literary criticism especially on the theme of expatriation. They have created a wide readership and a strong critical endorsement that reflect the attention of serious academics and scholars.

Mukherjee's fiction portrays expatriate characters and their experiences. As Jasbir Jain points out, "Mukherjee's novels are representative of the expatriate sensibility." (12) Her novels, *The Tiger's Daughter* and *Wife,* which I have chosen to analyze, deal with two different problems of expatriates. Both the novels portray how the immigrants in America try to adapt to the American culture and in consequence, are delineated as rootless. Mukherjee depicts the difficulties of the expatriates who are confused and desperate in breaking their ties with their native culture.

*The Tiger's Daughter* foregrounds the process of national construction through the trope of an expatriate's return to the ancestral homeland. It is the story of an expatriate's return to India in the hope of recovering her roots and the stability of her cultural identity as an Indian. In this novel, Mukherjee projects vividly through the experience of her protagonist, an Indian woman called Tara Banerjee Cartwright who is in Calcutta for a visit, the city she remembers. Tara, however, cannot help at the end wondering if it could be the home for her and the people there of her class. The central theme of this novel is the discovery of the heroine, Tara, that the city and the people she wanted to see after seven years' stay abroad were in a state of terminal decline, her growing awareness of her spirit of foreignness, and eventual realization that her future is in exploration only. Tara Banerjee-Cartwright is a postcolonial, elite, convent-educated, expatriate on a visit to India. An expatriate with dual affiliation, Tara's return to native land proves distressful and tragic. She encounters the clash of cultures and values in Calcutta. Hence, the westernized Tara feels like an expatriate in her own country. She is an expatriate who has lost her national and ethnic identity. At the end, she decides to return to her husband David in America. Instead of being comforted by middle-class Bengali Brahmin traditions, Tara is now struck by great impressions of poverty, hunger, disease, and political turmoil.

Sent by her father to New York at the age of fifteen, to pursue higher studies, Tara as a student faces discrimination on the alien soil. She feels homesick: "For Tara, Vassar had been an almost unsalvageable mistake . . . she would have rushed home to India at the end of first week." (10) At first, she finds it difficult to adjust to the alien culture, hence, her sense of loneliness. But with the exposure to American culture and its strangeness, she learns to develop qualities of courage, determination and strength. Tara's stay in America for seven years changes her attitude totally. She thinks on her own and gives importance to her desires. With this courage and determination, when she comes across cultural conflicts in America, she tries to resolve them herself. Whenever she confronts discrimination in the foreign land, she faces it boldly and reacts aggressively to defend her family and her native country instinctively when her friends try to ridicule it. Her prayer to goddess Kali to give strength to face the hardships in the alien land is an ample evidence to witness her longing for native culture. "She suffered fainting spells, headaches and nightmares. . . . She complained of homesickness in letters to her mother, who promptly prayed to Kali to save Tara's conscience, chastity and complexion." (13)

Expatriate's loneliness is reflected when her roommates have vacated for summer. Tara suffers from headaches and nightmares. She hangs silk scarves around her apartment to make it more Indian during times of her loneliness. Like any expatriate in a country like America, Tara creates a little India physically and emotionally without any communication whatsoever with the host culture.

During her stay for seven years in America, Tara's attitude is totally changed and she thinks on her own, gives importance to her desires and resolves the cultural conflicts in America faced by her. Overlooking her family customs, Indian culture and traditions, she takes a bold decision to marry an American David Cartwright, with whom she fell in love. Her family considers the marriage of Tara with David as breaking of Indian heritage. But Tara believes that her marriage with an American will give new meaning to her American life. Tara's American attitude to life is easily sensed by her relatives in India who find her "stubborn." Her American life evokes the dullness, emptiness and desperation caused due to the alienation and discrimination in the new land: "New York, she thought now, had been exotic. . . . There were policemen with dogs prowling the underground tunnels. Because girls like her . . . were being knifed in elevators in their own apartment buildings. . . . The only pollution she had been warned against in Calcutta had been caste pollution. New York was certainly extraordinary and it had driven her to despair." (33-34)

On her return to India after seven years, Tara finds herself a total stranger in the inherited milieu. She realizes that she is now neither Indian nor American. She is totally confused and lost in the tradition of an expatriate. Tara is apprehensive of the fact that her husband David Cartwright is wholly western. She cannot communicate with him the finer nuances of her family background and of life in Calcutta—the failure on her part is rooted in their cultural differences. In India a marriage is not simply a union of two individuals, it is a coming together of two families as well, unlike in America where a marriage is simply a contract between two individuals. David mistakes her love for family as over-dependence and whenever he asks questions about Indian customs and traditions, she fails to communicate its finer aspects, and she feels completely insecure in an alien atmosphere; Nagendra Kumar writes, "Madison square was unbearable and her husband was after all foreigner." (31) The cultural differences between Tara and David cause a feeling of insecurity in Tara. To overcome this feeling, she decides to visit India after a gap of seven years.

She has dreamt of her return to home country for several years and thought that all hesitations, and fears of her stay abroad would be erased magically on her return to Calcutta. The new Americanized Tara fails to bring back her old sense of perception and views India with the keenness of a foreigner. When her relatives address her as 'Tultul,' a nickname which they always used for her, it sounds strange to her Americanized ears. Seven years ago, Tara had admired "the houses on Marine Drive" (18) but her stay at Vassar has changed her outlook on Indian life. The very houses she admired then, "now their shabbiness appalled her" (18). After her return from America: "She feared their tone, their omissions, their aristocratic oneness." (43) After seeing Tara's negative reaction to the deterioration of Calcutta city, her friend Reena says that she has become "self-centred European." (105)

Tara experiences expatriation at all points of her life. Her relatives call her "*Americawali*" (42), and her husband "*mlec-cha*" (36). She feels that the Indians who show much interest for foreign things, dresses, do not approve marriage with foreign people.

Religion plays a vital role in any culture. When Tara forgets the rituals, it upsets her because she realizes that her westernization had made her oblivious of her religious traditions. Now she has become foreign to her native values also and it fills her with a sense of rootlessness. Tara begins to look at India as a land of poor people living in hostile, unhygienic conditions and suffering from starvation, disease and decay. When Tara visits Kananbala Mata Devi ashram at the request of her pious mother, she feels her soul uplifted by the *darshan* of Mata, forgetting all the hatred and wickedness for the time being. She experiences a sort of trance in the temple which is a typical religious experience: "Warm and persistent tears rose in Tara's heart. She forgot her instinctive suspicions, her fears of misunderstandings and scenes, she forgot her guardedness and atrophy in that religious moment. 'Ma, Ma, Mata!' she shouted with the rest" (173). Tara thus finds comfort and strength in her conscious returning to the rites and traditions of her religious faith.

While she was in America, Tara idealized her home country and cherishes its nostalgic memories. When she confronts the changed and hostile circumstances of her home country, all her dreams and ideals crumble down. Tara realizes that she was completely transformed by America. Her westernization has helped her view the wide gulf between the two worlds that cannot be bridged. In India she sees despair, disease, riot, poverty, beggars and children eating yogurt on the side walk. The climax of the novel is full of rapid and forceful incidents. The whole of Calcutta city is burning with violent protests and riots, and in the riots Tara's friend Pronob unfortunately gets killed by the mob. Mukherjee ends the novel with: "Tara, still locked in a car across the street from the Catelli-Continental, wondered whether she would ever get out of Calcutta, and if she did not, whether David would ever know that she loved him fiercely" (210). At the end Mukherjee keeps the mystery about the fate of Tara haunting the reader's mind in the sense of notion of alienation and expatriation what Tara experienced.

Mukherjee has clearly presented the cultural conflict of the East and the West in *The Tiger's Daughter*. Tara's attempt at assimilation in America ends in failure due to her otherness. She breaks her family tradition by marrying an American, only for security reasons in an alien land. But her marriage also proves a failure since she always remains nervous and apprehensive that her husband is a foreigner, and how well he would understand her and her Indian tradition. While in India, she feels alienated due to her changed outlook on Indian life after her seven years' stay in America. From the beginning to the end of the novel, Tara has been shown as shuttling between the world of alienation and the world of belonging—the Western world and the Indian world. She realizes that she is now neither Indian nor truly American. She is totally confused and lost. Throughout the novel she is shown as torn apart by the feeling of nostalgia, rootlessness and expatriation. Tara is caught between two contrasting cultures, and realizing that the gulf between the two worlds cannot be bridged, she decides to go back to her husband in America, her adopted homeland. There is a negotiation of her old identity being Hindu Brahmin woman—submissive, protected, dependent (on men), a subaltern, shy, gentle, obedient—and being American—white, Christian, an expatriate.

Bharati Mukherjee's novels portray the issues of the Indian and other Third World immigrants to tackle the problems of loss of culture, rootlessness and their endeavour to assume a new identity in the United States. Thus, *The Tiger's Daughter* portrays a complete sense of expatriation.

## Works Cited

Agrawal, Anju Bala. *Post-Independence Indian Writing in English*. New Delhi: Authors Press, 2008.

Agarwal, Beena. *Women Writers and Indian Diaspora*. New Delhi: Authors Press, 2011.

Akhilesh Barch and Nidhi Joshi, "Bharati Mukherjee's *The Tiger's Daughter* as a Study of an Immigrant's Psyche," *International Journal on Studies in English Language and Literature*, 4: 8, August 2016, pp. 37-40.

Bhatnagar, M.K. and M. Rajeshwar, ed. *Indian Writings in English* Vol. VI. New Delhi: Atlantic, 2000.

Edwards, Justin D. *Post Colonial Literature,* MacMillan, 2008.

Gauri Shankar Jha, *Current Perspectives in Indian English Literature*, Atlantic, 2006.

Inamdar, F.A. "Immigrant Lives: Protagonists in Bharati Mukherjee's *The Tiger's Daughter* and *Wife*," *Indian Women Novelists*, ed. R.K. Dhawan. New Delhi: Prestige, 1991. 187-201.

Indira, S. "Exploration of Inner Space: Anita Desai and Bharati Mukherjee," *Indian Women Novelists*, Set III: vol. 2.

Jaggi, Maya. "An Interview with Bharati Mukherjee," *Bazaar: South Asian Arts Magazine*, 13.8 (1990): 9.

Jasbir Jain, "Foreignness of Spirit: The World of Bharati Mukherjee's Novels," *The Journal of Indian Writings in English*, Vol. 13 (July 1985)12-18: 12.

Kumar, Nagendra. *The Fiction of Bharati Mukherjee: A Cultural Perspective,* New Delhi: Atlantic, 2001: 31

Meer, Ameena. "Bharati Mukherjee," *BOMB* 29 (1989): 18-29.

Mukherjee, Bharati. *The Tiger's Daughter*. New York: Fawcett, 1971.

Parameswaran, Uma. "Writing the Diaspora," *The Atlantic Library Review,* Vol. 1, No. 2, p. 165.

Patrica L. Sharpe, "The Challenge to the Indian Writer," *Quest*, 59 Autumn, 1968.

Sahoo, Ajaya Kumar and Brij Maharaj, ed. *Sociology of Diaspora*. Vol.1, New Delhi: Rawat, 2007.

Sheeba, K.G. "Analysis of Treatment of Immigrant Experience in Select Works of Bharati Mukherji," *Scholar Critic*, Vol. 2, Issue 1, April 2015, 145-53.

Singh, S.K. *The Great Indian Women Novelists in English Literature*. New Delhi: Mangalam, 2009.

Suchitra Patne, *A Study of Cultural and Psychological Conflicts in Bharati Mukherjee's Women Protagonists*. New Delhi, 2014.

# Diasporic Identity in the Novels of Kamila Shamsie

**VEENA LYDIA LOBO**
**Research Scholar, Mangalore University**

One of the challenges that people today face is the dilemma of identity. For Pakistan the concept of belonging, has a historical importance which is defined through the struggle for independence. Therefore Pakistani English literature acted as a medium through which national belonging found reflection. It is closely associated with an experience of immigration which is not merely geographical displacement but a displacement of culture, history and ideas that causes psychological imbalance and moral conflict. This painful experience finds its brilliant depiction in the writings of Nadim Aslam, Mohsin Hamid, Kamila Shamsie and many others. The confusion between native and alienation that exists at home and in society among the generations is discussed by these authors. There is a continuous development of novel as a leading form in Pakistani literature. When we look at Pakistani English Literature by the writers living in geographical borders of Pakistan and by Pakistani diasporic writers, we observe a multicultural milieu not only due to the fact that the writers represent different cultural backgrounds or because there is no other way of reflecting pluralist society like Pakistan, but because in their works these writers reach beyond ethno-linguistic, historical, religious and geographical confines.

As Neluka Silva asserts regarding the role of writing centred on female body in Pakistani society: "Writing about the body, breaking down its taboos, and soliciting individual freedom and self-realization by women, for women, has a clear political imperative within a landscape of religio-social repression and patriarchal authority, since the body is simultaneously a surface on which social law, morality values, and lived experiences are inscribed. Meanings are carved into and out of bodies." (208-9)

Kamila Shamsie is a Pakistani writer who is familiar with and at ease in many different countries and cultures. She lives in Karachi but spent part of her life in the West, mainly in the United States and in Great Britain. Kamila Shamsie's characters, who despite living on the same land she belongs to, face identity crises. As a result of social classes and cultural values which depict the notion that identity cannot be assumed by single factor rather it is of various aspects and is in continuous formation process. Identity crisis is the main theme of her novels, *Burnt Shadows* and *Kartography.* In *Burnt Shadows,* the author displays an interesting point of view with regard to the diasporic identity through the character of Hiroko, a Japanese girl, regarding the notion of belonging. Shamsie takes Hiroko through nuclear bombing in Nagasaki to war in Afghanistan and finally to New York where the 9/11 terror attack is experienced. She lost her fiancé in Nagasaki bomb blast and then she leaves that country and comes to India in 1947. She receives hospitality from her fiancé's stepsister and later marries a man named Sajjad. Both of them move to Pakistan, it was the most crucial time of the partition. At the end of the story Hiroko moves to United States, to escape the danger of an atomic conflict in the subcontinent and there she witnesses the September 2001 terrorist attack on the World Trade Centre. So her story narrated experiences such as the loss of homeland and foreignness. By depicting all these incidents in her novel Shamsie narrates how violence caused the same pain and how the various events get interrelated through their effect on personalities belonging to different nations and the idea of belonging loses its primary importance in the struggle of survival. Hiroko displays the similar nature of such categories like national belonging and that makes it possible for her to live through all struggles in her life, and to survive. Hiroko symbolizes those people whose lives are spent in migration from one region to another. Compromising the social and cultural differences in a marginal dimension, which corresponds to Homi Bhabha's concept of 'third space,' allows questioning the dominant narratives. In *Burnt Shadows,* the third space produced by the protagonist's agency, where she negotiates her identity in resistance to certain social rules, can be seen as simultaneous with the transnational space. It is Hiroko's agency which makes her move nation- states which makes her an in- between and has to negotiate with her identity in relation to different languages and various cultural and social positions. Kamila Shamsie feels exclusively as the part of Karachi, as she herself expresses in her novel *Kartography,* "will always be a Karachiwallah." The major theme of the novel is displacement due to the violence in Karachi. The novel has the political sketches of 1971 and moves around the issues of politics and identity. She validates the fact that political issues and government policies affect the lives of people and create problems in the society:

> I caught my parents exchanging worried glances. "What a silly remark, Ali," my mother said.
>
> "What's silly about it? The factory area is still under curfew."

Through this novel she brings out the fact how people are known by the politics of their nation. The year 1971 witnessed a phenomenon in Pakistan, namely civil war. The war brought division of united Pakistan and created a new nation Bangladesh. It brought about horror, chaos, murders, theft and divisions. Although the novel appears to be a tale of two families, a saga of love, sacrifice and separation of friends but at the base of the family struggles laid the issues of political polity and personal identity. It is the policy of creation of East and West Pakistan that caused the trauma and pain to the family members of Raheen and Karim. During childhood, Raheen is close to Karim as if like twins, rather than the only son of her parent's best friends. Later they were romantically interested in each other and their parents hoped that they would marry. But due to the outbreak of violence in Karachi they were separated and Karim's parents moved to London for better safety. Raheen tries to keep contact with Kareem, where the latter shows indifferent attitude towards her and becomes obsessed with what he calls "kartograhy," as if by mapping his world, he could gain some control over his own fate. Especially the impact on the city Karachi is inevitable. Whatever is happening in Karachi does not limit to the city itself but affects the entire nation and national issues. The whole novel is about Karachi. What Shamsie conveys through this novel is that love for one's home, one's city and one's homeland is a natural feeling shared by all. But the experience of diaspora varies from person to person and the context in which it occurs. The anxiety of leaving the home land and resettling in an unknown set up is the part of diaspora's traumatic experience. As the physical separation divides the bond of relationship so also the emotional feelings, the pangs of pain have a lot to do in diaspora.

Kamila Shamsie's two novels articulate the problem of identity as well as the complexity of the country's political issues and the present situation. She is well-versed in the art of characterization. Her diasporic writing bears much relevance to the contemporary society which is torn by differences and conflicts.

## Bibliography

Ahmed, Z. 'Pakistani Feminist Fiction and the Empowerment of Women.' *Pakistaniaat*: *A Journal of Pakistan Studies.*

Albrow, M. and E. King, *Globalization, Knowledge, and Society*. London: Sage, 1990.

Bhabha, Homi, K. *The Location of Culture*. New York: Routledge, 1994.

Brah, Avtar. *Cartographies of Diaspora: Contesting Identities*. Routledge, 1996.

Chaudhary, F. *Hiding and Seeking Identity: The Female Figure in the Novels of Pakistani Female Writers in English: A Feminist Approach*. Unpublished Doctoral Diss., Univ. of Huddersfield, U.K. http: //eprints.hud.ac.uk/17563 March, 2013.

Cilano, C.N. *Contemporary Pakistani Fiction in English: Idea, Nation, State*, London: Routledge, 2013.

_____. *National Identities in Pakistan: The 1971 War in Contemporary Pakistani Fiction*. New York, 2014.

Celt, Adrienne. "War and Pieces: Review of Shamsie's *Burnt Shadows*," *The Huffington Post*. http: //www.huffingtonpost.com.

Harish, Trivedi, et. al. *The Nation across the World: Postcolonial Literary Representations*. OUP, 2007.

Itakura, G., "A Lanky Shadow on the Rock: Trauma in Kamila Shamsie's *Burnt Shadows*," *4th Global Conference: Trauma Theory and practice, Prague, Czech Republic*. Cambridge: MIT Press, 2014.

Shamsie, Kamila. *Kartography*. London: Bloomsbury, 2002.

_____, *Burnt Shadows*. London: Bloomsbury, 2009.

Shamsie, Muneeza, ed. *Leaving Home: Towards a New Millennium: A Collection of English Prose by Pakistani Women*. Karachi: OUP, 2001.

Silva, Neluka. *The Gendered Nation. Contemporary Writings from South Asia*. New Delhi, 2004.

# Reading Mahasweta Devi's *Mother of 1084* in the Dichotomy of Death

**SHIRIN AKTER POPY**
**Noakhali Science and Technology University, Bangladesh**

Mahasweta Devi (1926-2016) as a writer and socio-political activist felt a moral obligation to herself and her times. In fact, this obligation indulges her to give voice to the peasants, outcastes, untouchables, tribal and young idealists who stood either against the exploitive system of the government or against the societal malpractices. *Mother of 1084* written against the backdrop of the Naxalite movement is such a voice per se. This award-winning novel, apart from being a psychological journey of a bereaved mother (Sujata) pondering over the memories of her dead son (Brati), is a mirror of the use of Repressive State Apparatus—weapons, torture, violence and killings—as a response to the resistance. Besides evoking the brutal killings of the Naxalites, Devi "concentrates on the later reactions and lack of reaction of a cross-section of the survivors, both those who bear the scars and wounds literally and figuratively of those horrible days and those who had lived through the days of violence in simulated insularity" (Bandyopadhyay xiv). The present paper is an attempt to look closely at the novel from the varied ways these survivors are taken into account—while some are shown to be dying, some are referred to as dead on several occasions. Moreover, focusing on the characters, the paper seeks to reread the novel from the dichotomy between corporal and spiritual death.

*Mother of 1084* apparently begins with a quest of "an apolitical mother . . . to know her martyred Naxalite son, to know what he stood for" (Bandyopadhyay xii)) but, as the story unfolds, it gradually steps into the untrodden realm of the so-called upper class society not only to peep into the frivolity of their familial relations but also to expose the hypocrisy and immorality lying underneath the flamboyance of their aristocracy. Knowing Dibyanath Chatterjee, from Devi's picture, is a harrowing experience as he is neither a good husband nor an ideal father. Dibyanath's character as an unfeeling one gets expressed in his reaction to the news of his youngest son's death. Though it is a truth, universally acknowledged, that the loss of a child is the most tragic event in the life of a parent. Instead of being broken in grief, Dibyanath attempted to hide the news of Brati's killing from any news report, in fear of losing his place and security in the society he belongs to. The news of Brati's death might have been a relieving one for his father because unlike his other children Brati was an obstacle to his erotic rendezvous. His attitude to dead Brati, officially shows the death of his fatherly instincts. In this point, Somu's father can be considered as a foil to Dibyanath. While Dibyanath wanted to erase the trace of dead Brati, Somu's father stepped ahead to die first before anybody can kill his son. He tried to save Somu. He went to police station, fell at the feet of the police officers and pleaded for their help to save his son. Failing to rescue Somu, he expected justice at least. However, it ended up in sheer hopelessness and a desperate cry: "O God! There is no justice in this country!" (67). He is not a rich man like Dibyanath. In fact, he is "a poor shopkeeper who had no capital," (66) but as a father his love for his son was so profound that the brutal death of Somu before his eyes caused his untimely death. In Devi's words, "the two fathers . . . lived in the same country, but poles apart" (66). In fact, here lies the basic difference between the two fathers depicted in the novel: one lives appropriating money, power and politics and the other, believing in law, justice and basic human goodness, died betrayed.

Dibyanath's turning a deaf ear to Sujata's wailing and maltreatment of Sujata also proves him to be an irresponsible husband. All through her life, Sujata was used as a child-bearing machine and a sexual object. In spite of being the father of four grown-up children, Dibyanath "had always fooled around with women," (31) considering it an act of virility. As a husband he is immoral, infidel, and an emblem of patriarchy.

Devi continues to lash at the upper class inhumanity through her characterization of Jyoti, Neepa and Tuli—Dibyanath's other children. Jyoti's loyalty and obedience to his father exhibits his alliance with the bleak, morbid and immoral culture of his time. In every way, he helped his father to wipe out Brati's existence from their memory. After the death of his youngest brother, instead of trying to unearth the cause of his brother's faithlessness and rejection to "the society ruled by profit-mad businessmen and leaders blinded by self-interest," (19) he got engaged in justifying the killing and trying to convince his mother that Brati was the worst criminal among all other criminals in the society. Joyti's unfailing support to his father clearly indicates that like his father he belongs to "the killers in the society, those who adulterated food, drugs and baby food . . . the leaders who led the people to face guns of police and found for themselves the safest shelters under police protection" (19)—"that Brati and his comrades had tried to exterminate" (115).

The apathetic human nature of this period is more exemplified through Tuli's character. Tuli is so insensitive and heartless to her mother's feelings that she and others set the date of her engagement with the "master swindler" (31) on Brati's death anniversary. Moreover, instead of being compassionate to her mother's grief, she supported her father's unrestrained sexuality. She was the first member in the family "to know about

Dibyanath's mistress, the typist. But she kept it a secret. She hadn't felt dislike or disgust for Dibyanath [rather] . . . she drew a strange sense of gratification and pride out of this" (96-97). Tuli's sense of ethics is clear in her defence to Dibyanath's infidelity as an escape from unhappiness. Tuli even epitomizes her father as the icon of a 'virile man.' With conviction she sometimes asserted that "if one married, one should marry only a man like him" (97). In fact, the authoritativeness, infidelity and carelessness of Dibyanath made him an epitome of virility to Tuli. Undoubtedly, it's her crippled morality that makes her father a role model to her. Her support to her father's authoritativeness and infidelity exemplifies her ethical standing and clarifies how these people are "contaminated and diseased from the very womb" (115).

In Devi's depiction, Neepa's marriage to Amit once again brings forth the frivolity of conjugal relationship. Neepa agreed to marry Amit—a weak-spirited, cowardly, pampered son of a rich father" (114) —only to exploit him and his riches so that she can live a life of luxury at ease. Her blatant shamelessness epitomizes that she is the female version of Dibyanath. She is both flamboyant and bold at her betrayal. She cuckolded her husband under his nose. "There was a time when [Amit] did not drink at all. But now he drank to get drunk. . . . Amit began drinking after Neepa began to live with his cousin in his house" (114-15). Actually she is shown to be an emblem of moral and sexual degeneration enjoying an epicurean life on her husband's wealth and in the sexual adventure with his cousin. Neepa often drives the nearby road of her parental home, but never comes to visit her mother and others. Her apathy and callousness to her mother and other siblings overtly ascertains her place in the society of the deceased where "the dead pretended to live within relationships that were long dead and thus keep up a masquerade of life" (115).

In his famous play *Hamlet*, Shakespeare adores human beings thus: "What a piece of work is man. How noble in reason, how infinite in faculty, in form and moving, how express and admirable, in action how like an Angel, in apprehension, how like a god. The beauty of the world!" (II.ii.883). If rationality, virtue, justness, apprehension, emotion are the emblem of human beings that separates them from other living creatures, the absence of these qualities is a mark of death, if not physical then spiritual of course. In her depiction of the wealthy Chatterjee family, a deep-rooted spiritual death is very prominent. Through Sujata's realization that "if Brati drank like Jyoti, if he could go about drunk like Neepa's husband, if he could flirt with the slip of a typist the way Brati's father did, if he could be as loose as his sister Neepa, who lived with a cousin of her husband," (31) Brati might have got the license to live.

While Sujata was trying to know the real Brati, the dead Brati is re-evoked in the narrativization of Somu's mother and Nandini, which demystifies the causes of Brati's involvement with the state-forbidden movement. In "A Tryst with Destiny," *Jawaharlal Nehru,* the first Prime Minister of India, promised "to bring freedom and opportunity to the common man, to the peasants and workers of India; to fight and end poverty and ignorance and disease; to build up a prosperous, democratic and progressive nation, and to create social, economic and political institutions which will ensure justice and fullness of life to every man and woman."

However, during the Indian Government under Jawaharlal Nehru "despite certain obvious outward changes in forms of governance . . . [it] represented in many respects a continuation of British attitudes both in form and substance" (Das 7). Moreover, there was no such positive change in the existing class and caste tensions. Consequently, claiming justice, people's revolts against the ruling system have occurred frequently. The emergence of the Naxalites during the Seventies is a case in point. The movement broke out in the northern West Bengal, in May 1967. The causes of the movement are "in essence socio-economic" and political because the "spirit of the law remained confined to paper and the people were let to languish" (Dixit 23). Brati and thousands like him got disillusioned with the false promises of the government. Brati knows all the anguishes of Somu, Laltu, Bijit, Partha—all the brilliant sons of poor fathers. They were disappointed by life itself. The economic deprivation and exploitation of the oppressed class forced them to rise against all the establishments. In Devi's narratives, the rebels fight against injustice, inequality, suppression and die for the cause of humanity. In *Mother of 1084,* she depicts such a society and time where men like Brati have been denied the rights to live and in an orgy of violence thousands of them have been wiped out altogether. They are reduced to nothing but to numbers. In the Chatterjee family Devi depicted, the only member who had the basic human essentials to assert moral, social and ideological points in a snappy, narcissistic, feudal and superficial society, had to die an unnatural death because he lived in a society that "gave the dead the right to live, and denying it to the living" (115).

Devi, in *Mother of 1084,* points a finger at the moral standing of the community, society and the time itself. She points out how prison walls were being raised higher everyday to accommodate the increasing number of so-called rebels. Labelling them as terrorists, everyday thousands of country's youths were wiped out. In spite of observing these carnages, the psyche of the upper class people remains undisturbed and unaffected. These people are either consciously unconscious or they have no consciousness at all. Their lives are lived only in the enclave of their self-interest and self-centredness. Through Sujata's disappointment Devi expresses her disgust in a comment: "what a city to live in . . . where such horrors could take place, and the routine of cultural festival and fairs dedicated to the poet Tagore could continue unaffected" (63). The novel depicts such a society where the upper class people were heedless and apathetic towards human suffering and distress. Neither do they try to know the causes behind the upsurge, nor do they seek to find the reasons for the extermination of the youths. They are happy in their shells and pleased to go to their clubs everyday because this is the way they find meaning in their survival. Through execution of the youths, police officers like Saroj Pal get early promotions. It is ironical that after the death of Brati, the friends of Chatterjee family come to offer condolences not on the loss of the son but rather feeling "how hard he [Brati's father] worked to hush things up!" (112). Thus Devi finds "the entire social system cadaverous" (Bandyopadhyay viii) where Dibyanaths, Saroj Pals and betrayers like Anindya have all the rights to live in with pride and authority.

Death comes as a metaphor in *Mother of 1084*. Devi, here, sheds light on how the melodramatic death of Somu, Partha and others, on stage, caused their families to die every day behind the curtain. The death of Partha made his mother collapse. And his brother, due the fear of being arrested, takes refuge at his aunt's place. He cannot get back to normal life because his brother had placed "absolute faith in the cult of faithlessness" (20). The consequence of Somu's death is heart-rending. His death resulted in a 'life-in-death' situation for his family members. Bearing the burden of poverty, his mother grows paler day by day. Her life is nothing better than death as Devi comments, "Her appearance carried the look of death" (58). Somu's sister couldn't continue her studies because she had to devote herself to support her family. Since the death of Somu, she was trying hard to run the household by giving tuition from dawn to dusk. But with her meagre income, she could hardly manage their survival. She aspires for a technical job but gets rejected every time because she is Somu's sister and it is foreshadowed that she will never get a job. Somu's father died out of grief, and his mother and sister are dying every day due to poverty, negligence and hopelessness. In fact, "Somu's dying had left [them] dead" (35).

In the twentieth century iconoclast poem, *The Waste Land*, T.S. Eliot depicted a spiritually degenerated modern generation with all its vices, lust and greed. To denote the absence of purity, sanctity and holiness in the modern western cities, in contrast to the early spiritual justness, Eliot writes: *"He who was living is now dead./* We who were living are now dying" (328-29) Thus, Eliot propagates that the crucifixion of Christ is the killing of values and when values are lost in the living people, they are the walking dead only. Like the spiritually dead people depicted in the poem, Mahasweta Devi in *Mother of 1084*, not only draws the picture of a family where all relationships are long dead, but also portrays a dead society where institutions are perpetrating exploitation, violence and execution on anybody questioning its hollowness and injustice. The novel ends with Sujata's emergence into existence from her long unresponsive and non-existent self. However, the moment she exploded against almost all the members of the family, her appendix bursts out suggesting an impending death. Devi, in the end, puts Sujata into a purposeful paradox—where her psychic regeneration leads her to physical deterioration—to signify the contradiction of the time that one loses the right to live physically immediately after one rises against the dead morals of the society.

## Works Cited

Bandyopadhyay, Samik. Introduction to *Mother of 1084*.

Das, Suranjan. "The Nehru Years in Indian Politics," *Edinburgh Papers in South Asian Studies*, 16 (2001): 2-35.

Devi, Mahasweta. *Mother of 1084*, trans. Samik Bandyopadhyay. Calcutta: Seagull, 2011.

Dixit, Raman. "Naxalite Movement in India: The State's Response," *Journal of Defence Studies*, 4.2 (2010): 21-35.

Eliot, T.S. *The Waste Land*. New York: W.W. Norton, 2001.

Nehru, Jawaharlal. "A Tryst with Destiny," *Great Speeches of the 20th Century*, Guardian News and Media Limited, 1 May 2007.

Shakespeare, William. *Hamlet. William Shakespeare Complete Works*, ed. W.J. Craig, London: Oxford University Press, 1966.

# Portrayal of Women in Kannada Theatre

**THAMMAIAH R.B.**
**Padmashree Institute of Management & Sciences, Bangalore**
**D.K. PRABHAKAR**
**Department of Telugu, Bangalore University**

The history of feminism in India can be divided into three phases: the first phase, beginning in the mid-nineteenth century, initiated when male European colonists began to speak out against the social evils of Sati; the second phase, from 1915 to Indian independence, when Gandhi incorporated women's movements into the Quit India Movement and independent women's organizations began to emerge; and finally, the third phase, post-independence, which has focused on fair treatment of women in the work force and right to political parity.

The concept of gender is an important one which pervades the disciplines of literature, cultural studies, film studies and in theatre as well. Feminism is a significant ideology, fast developing in the modern times. It emerged as a concept in the west with the objective of providing a space for women in the society, later on embracing the superb ideas of an egalitarian society, where the dialectics of male dominance and female subordination are erased. Having started as a social movement, it became a discourse, wielding a formidable influence on world literature. A woman has become the centre of discussion in the postcolonial literature and social strata of India as well as western countries. The lives of women have been manipulated by the patriarchy in all ages and cultures, undoubtedly in different ways by prescribing values, norms, gender roles and ethics to keep the male dominance at the top.

In the recent years, people have become increasingly attentive to gender issues, cross-examining the relationship of women to nationalism and modernity in the dramatic sphere. Kannada theatre has played a revolutionary role in bringing changes in society in terms of behaviour and culture. Women expressions, actions, or roles are perceived as a commodity for artistic or cultural consumption. There have been a few path-breaking plays in Kannada in the past. Kannada has always voiced the concerns of the marginalised. But there have been different attempts by different groups to break free from this kind of unarticulated oppression and create space for the hitherto neglected and marginalised sections. The established generation of Karnad, Kambara and Lankesh wrote new plays often departing from earlier methods. Talented younger playwrights like H.S. Shivaprakash also appeared in the limelight.

Chandrashekara Kambara is an outstanding playwright, poet, folklorist, film director in Kannada language and also one of the prominent playwrights in modern Kannada theatre. His plays are the searching tools to new stages of his creative passions and impressions. We have to notice the thing that folk culture and the modernism come across in the combined form.

The Sirisampige stands equally with the Kannada plays like *Hayavadana*, *Nagamandala*, *Sangyabalya*. In *Sirisampige*, he has done the same thing by using the folklore to present the theme of conflict between body and mind and search and split of self. He dealt with these themes through the characters such as Shivanaga and Kalinga; Avali and Javali entertain the audience by showing their lack of independent existence. All these characters invariably depend on one another to live. In the play the story of the prince develops itself in a dignified look and took the mode as a tragedy play, where as the sub-sequent stories took a comic verse presenting the style of a *prahasana*. In the play the main female roles are of Mayavati, Sirisampige, Deepadamolle and Kamala. The dilemma of the woman is portrayed in such a way that it never appears to be vulgar or indecent. The subaltern status was prescribed only for women.

*Jokumaraswami* is another play of Kambara to demonstrate the patriarchy and its impact on the lives of women. In this play, the women characters expose and oppose patriarchal oppression. The play describes the patriarchal society which sustains conceptual framework that maintains structures of domination. He regards women and nature as irrational beings that are present to be dominated and exploited for the needs of man. Patriarchal society sustains false notions about men and keeps them blind to their real side. By the wisdom of ages, Shari and Ningi in *Jokumaraswami* examine the weakness and hypocrisy of men and stand evidence to the fact that women are more perceptive than men. And they examine the patriarchal systems of domination that oppress women and reveal the false ideologies of patriarchy. Further, these women have strong concern for nature and claim its intrinsic value and inherent worth. By showing the representation of patriarchy in religious practices and the fashioning of gods, the playwright points out its consequence and calls for a new religion that acknowledges the contribution of women. He explains the shortcomings of conceptual structures and places women at the centre of discussion. The entire play describes feminist studies that persist on the need for revolution in the social and economic structures that exploit women. The difficulties faced by women, the horrors they are subjected to, the discrimination, the suppression they suffer at the hands of men.

Girish Karnad is a playwright, poet, actor, director and translator. He wrote in Kannada and later translated his plays into English. Karnad effectively demonstrated how Indian English drama could revitalize itself by employing native, soil-related subjects. He wrote in Kannada which shows that his soul remained indigenous. He wrote a number of plays such as *Yayati*, *Tughlaq*, *Hayavadana*, *Naga-Mandala* and *Tale-Danda*.

Karnad's concern for the oppressed and the weak led him to the espousal of women's cause and his plays are saturated with a spirit of gender justice and feminism. *Hayavadana* elevated women on a pedestal higher than that of the man. Its theme was borrowed from *Kathasaritasagar*, a collection of Sanskrit stories. It has a complicated, bizarre plot consisting of two close friends Devdatta and Kapila. Devdatta was an intellectual and Kapila a man of body who represent two extreme opposites—one Apollonian; another Dionysian tendency. Devdatta married Padmini but she fell in love with Kapila which created a compellingly unbearable situation for both the friends who consequently committed suicide out of remorse. Padmini has no choice except to immolate herself with her husband's dead body in a sati ceremony. This act of self-immolation by sitting on the funeral pyre of her dead husband shows the agony and pitiable plight of women in India. Karnad's treatment of this episode shows the tyranny of religious and social conventions relating exclusively to women which consider marriage as the supreme boon of woman who achieves salvation through her services to her male protector—the husband.

Padmini, in *Hayavadana,* is also in a similar plight. Though not accused by anybody in the play as immoral or anti-social, she is almost blamed of adultery. She marries Devadatta and falls in love with Kapila, her husband's friend. Devadatta is the epitome of all intellectuality and Kapila of physicality. Padmini will never be complete without either of them. Her desire to have both men does not look immoral or unnatural. The dilemma of the woman is portrayed in such a way that it never appears to be vulgar or indecent. The evil custom of sati was enjoined on the women so that even after the death of her husband she remained chaste and did not go to any other man. The fact that the man after his wife's death was not expected to immolate himself and could get another spouse shows the extent of gender injustice in India. The subaltern status was prescribed only for women.

In *Hayavadana*, It exhibits the existential anguish and predicament even of liberated women in contemporary Indian society. Woman is shown to have the liberty to carry on her affair with another man which results in the suicide of her husband as also her paramour and yet she is not fully liberated. Padmini indulges in an extra-marital relationship but does not express her desires openly. By supernatural aid, both these women are able to satiate their desires.

Padmini is a complex woman who is not ashamed to be in love with two men, her husband and his friend. The play is about incompleteness, imperfection in life. It begins with an invocation to Lord Ganesha who is an embodiment of imperfection himself with broken tusk, elephant head, seated on mouse, snake around belly etc. The play poses the question of imperfection through Devadatta and Kapila who symbolize intellectuality and physicality respectively. But the play stands out by the view it adopts towards Padmini who wants them both. The female chorus in the play asks: "why should love stick to the sap of a single body?" The chorus sings as if they speak for Padmini: "a head for each breast. A pupil for each eye. A side for each arm. I have neither regret nor shame." Nowhere in the play is Padmini condemned or criticized for her action which is surprising even from a modern point of view. Her wish to live and love both lives is accepted and treated as if it is natural. Neither the Bhagavatha nor the chorus nor any other character in the play says anything about Padmini's seemingly immoral actions.

Karnad's women take care of their desires and to achieve them find their own way. Karnad portrays the way marriages are fixed in India. Padmini, though an enchanting woman, wages a war against the patriarchal order of command and ultimately she too becomes a prey to the tyranny of the patriarchal society. It is the undeniable reality that Indian culture considers marriage to be the supreme blessing for a woman, because it offers her salvation through her service to her husband. For her, chastity is superior and preferable to life itself. But, she denied love, enjoyment, entertainment and freedom, which are indispensable to the growth of her personality.

In *The Heap of Broken Images* Manjula indirectly suggests that her husband had an affair with her sister. One day she comes home at an unexpected time and enters the room stealthily. The two were discussing the merits and demerits of Electronics and Human Heritage. They were shocked by her arrival. Their faces reminded her of the couples' gaze when they were caught in the act of love. Malini due to her physical debacle cannot move out of her house. She is restricted to a wheel chair. Pramod, because of his career in software, need not move out of the house. Due to their like-mindedness they share many topics in the absence of Manjula Naik. So she used to call him 'Tirupathi Thimmappa' suggesting a man who leads his life happily with two women. Manjula feels subordinated in many respects. In her childhood her parents showed extra care to this girl and they arranged special tuitions for her. As she was a brilliant girl she could grasp the things very well. Manjula spells out her opinion: "I would have been a better person had I been given encouragement like Malini." The very statement exposes her inferiority to Malini. Manjula, from the beginning, craved for an identity. She aspires for a sort of recognition at home and later in the world. At last a new identity is formed out of transmutation of situations. In the field of Indian drama Karnad's experiment, though puzzling at first, is innovative and may trigger many new experiments besides new vistas in the world of criticism.

It is a new way that these dramatists look at their women characters. It is not mere sympathy. It is not mere ideological support. It is more a claim from within, internal to the dramatist. It is almost like a woman writing these works. The difficulties faced by women, the horrors they are subjected to, the discrimination, the suppression they suffer at the hands of men – all these are so well depicted that it all appears to have flown naturally from a woman's hand. And, instead of a loud clamour for rights and justice, there is a very strong, clear but calm assertion of women's position.

## Works Cited

Annaiah Gowda, H.H., ed. "Contemporary Kannada Drama," *Indian Drama*, (Mysore, MU, 1974).

Baraguru Ramachandrappa, ed. "Chandrashekara Kambarara Sahithydalli Janapada Tantra," "Kambarara Sahithydalli Pouranika Asayagalu," "Nanna Bhaduku Bharaha," *Hosahathushahi Anubhava mattu Kambarara Sahithya* (Bangalore: Karnataka Sahitya Akademi, 1992).

Amur G.S., ed. *Kannada Theatre, A Crisis in Sensibility, Images and Impressions; Essays mainly on Contemporary Indian Literature* (Jaipur: Panchasheela, 1979).

Girish Karnad, Author's Introduction, *Three Plays by Girish Karnad*, (Madras: OUP, 1995).

Narasimhaiah C.D. and C.N. Srinath, ed. "A Note on *Hayavadana*," *Literary Criterion.*

Rangacharya, Adya. Opening Scene: Early Memoirs of a Dramatist and a Play (New Delhi: Penguin, 2006).

Ranganath, H.K. *Karnataka Rangabhoomi*. Bangalore: Kannada Pustaka Pradhikaara, 2000 (1978).

Vaidyanathan T.G., Introduction, *Sirisampige*, by C Kambara (Calcutta: Seagull, 1992).

# Space in Vaidehi's Stories

**SOWMYA B.V.**

**Government First Grade College, Shikaripura, Dt. Shimoga**

Space represents an author's model of the world, expressed in the language of spatial representation. Spatial setting is a fundamental component of narration and therefore has always been a subject of narratological studies. The first person to approach the issue of literary space from the semiotic point of view was Yuri Lotman, a Russian, semiotician and cultural historian. He said that space organizations are governed by cultural stereotypes and conventions. Januz Stawinski a Polish philologist considered that there are three fundamental space modelling codes. The presented reality is the most fundamental code modelling space. Literary/ cultural conventions constitute the second space-modelling code. Language is the last of codes shaping space. These codes organize space in a way, define it, and provide terms for various types of spatial arrangements.

Until recently space was neglected in favour of time as parameter of literary analysis. Space in literary fiction was often considered to have no other function than to supply a general background against which the action takes place. From the end of the twentieth century onwards, however, space has become a 'hot topic' in literary studies. Space is no longer viewed as static or inert background action, but as an agent that shapes ideas, beliefs, principles and values. Modern spatial theorists understand space as dynamic, relational agent touching every arena of social and cultural life.

This paper discusses the treatment of space in Vaidehi's stories as an active agent in the shaping of stories and influencing the human characters. The space in Vaidehi's stories mostly consists of a small town or a village, kitchen, and some places surrounding a house. This space is completely filled with patriarchal beliefs. Women here live within the fence bound by the society. The language used by the people here and the description of the space also suggest a particular geographical area. It represents the cultural conventions of the area. In these places women characters suffer, cry, laugh, live, compromise and also rebel. In this space women live their life: some suffering, some compromising, and some even enjoy in spite of sufferings. We also find some women find their self-identity and struggle to get out of that space. The above observations are illustrated in this paper through Vaidehi's stories.

Vaidehi (Janaki Srinivas Murthy), born in 1945, in Kundapura, Dakshina Kannada District, Karnataka, is a well-known Kannada writer, renowned for her fight for the cause of women. Her writings, generally described as postmodernist, depict the plight of women in an indignant and rebellious tone. After doing her B.Com. in Kundapur, Vaidehi married K.L. Srinivas Murthy and went to live in Shimoga. They later moved to Udupi and went to Manipal. Vaidehi has received many prestigious awards. This year she was awarded Kannada Rajyothsava Award. She has also received Karnataka Sahitya Akademi Award, the M.K. Indira Award and the Katha Award. Many of her works have been translated into English and many Indian languages. She has also got Kendra Sahitya Akademi Award for her collection of short stories *Krouncha Pakshigalu* in 2009.

The spaces of Vaidehi's stories resemble her native. The language used by the characters, the geological descriptions, the customs, traditions and cultural life described in her stories resemble the Space of Dakshina Kannada. 'Patrode,' a dish of Dakshina Kannada, is a favourite food of her characters. In the story 'Kola' Khande Rao silks and Gandhi Bazaar suggest the town Shimoga.

Vaidehi was born and brought up in a large family which had many children and had relatives and friends visiting every day. Vaidehi says about her writing in *Gulabi Talkies and Other Stories*. "For women of those days staying indoors was a habit. If there were menfolk sitting on the veranda women were not supposed to go there. Women were not even allowed to speak loudly. If some woman talked loudly they would peep out curiously and would exclaim 'Who's that? Speaking loudly like a man?'" (xiii). The girls were not allowed to sit on chairs. Only men used to sit on chairs and read the newspapers. Girls did not go anywhere except school. And at home, they had many chores to occupy them. She says: "the serving of food an ever-readiness to be hospitable was a permanent feature of our inner world . . . what did we have except work and more work? Reading, writing, singing all these were for later" (xiii). Vaidehi is known to have announced: "Kitchen is my guru; that's where I learned many lessons."

Vaidehi was influenced by many women who lived around her in her real life. She says: "and so I grew up, watching women like Kamala, Krishni, Seethu, Lakshmi and others, those without husbands, those whose husbands were barely there, husbands who had gone away over the ghats and started another family, husbands who had descended from the heavens to join the family but who could disappear at any moment. All these women lived amidst sorrow and poverty, but with great strength. They overcame their helplessness in their own ways and took heart so that they could live" (xviii). As a writer Vaidehi says that her desire is to achieve in her writing the balance she had heard about in the inner world of the home. As Vaidehi herself puts it, there is a clear demarcation between the outside world; with its loud authoritative voices and the inside world with its silences. Still women of her stories try to resist the world but ultimately they end up submitting to exploitative society, resigning themselves to their fate. They are taught from childhood to suppress their feelings, to conceal their emotions and to withhold their real selves from society. Parents find a sense of achievement in marrying off their daughters. Ritual of marriage reduces girls to a mere object. Most women remain within domestic sphere. Hence most of their problems are also related to domestic life. That's why spaces in Vaidehi's stories are mostly home in a village with all its patriarchal conventions. Let's look at the stories where women suffered in patriarchy.

In 'Sougandhi's Soliloquies,' Sougandhi wants something exciting and thrilling to happen in her life. She comes to a town away from her native place. Parents are over-protective about their daughter. They are afraid to leave her alone there. "In the midst of all this, Sougandhi existed, nursing the small hope that before she lost her voice altogether she could go away to a distant place. So finally she had been able to come away, to a different town, to a different house. Here there was just the house, and herself. No one else. She could push the world aside and live her life. . . . Now she was a bird which had escaped from the palace beyond the seven gated fortress" (110). But her landlady and her parents do not let Sougandhi enjoy her freedom. Sougandhi says: "how difficult it was to say—leave me alone" (111). "Saugandhi's sorrow never boiled over. It always simmered" (115). She says: "My mind seems to have become wooden. . . . perhaps it's frozen" (115). She too desires men to look at her. But "she was from a respectable family. . . . She wanted to lose the mask of deceit . . . to shed hypocrisy" (116). It is shocking to see the contrast in Sougandhi's external modest and chaste appearance and her inner fantasies.

The story 'Antarangada Putagalu' focuses on an Indian woman's feelings of isolation and alienation both within and outside the marriage. The story focuses on 'Achala's Marriage,' who is carried away by romantic illusions about marriage. She goes on rejecting the suitors; one after another saying, "I never saw that bright ray of light in anybody's eyes. I didn't feel that intense desire to bear his child" (133). Achala asks Venkata sarcastically: "Well, all you need is a girl, just like a fan, fridge, table, utensils and site—don't you?" (139) to which Venkata retorts, "Why do you say that? What more do the girls need?" (139). The housemaid Subbi daringly gives birth to a child without getting married. Achala desires to live like Subbi.

The story 'Puttamatthe and Her Granddaughter' is a story of Puttamatthe struggling hard to live a respectable life. It was such a world where a woman was not supposed to talk loudly to her husband. Puttamatthe's mother was thrown into the well because she replied to her husband. A woman's self-respect is considered arrogance. Just like her mother Puttamatthe is also a woman of self-respect. "She was the kind who was inclined to think that a well-spent day was a day where she did not have to feel ashamed of herself" (143). She says to her granddaughter: "Child, this is how the world functions. Life is not what you and I expect it to be. . . . It is our responsibility to lead a respectable life." The difficulties of her life have made her tough and a great philosopher too. She says: "There is no one who doesn't have hunger and thirst. But all the desire is here—in this heart. If you harden this, all traces of desire will dry up soon." Thus she tries to live her life respectfully in spite of hardships of patriarchal society. Kamalavathi, her granddaughter, is a young, ambitious girl. She is not a passive victim like her grandmother. She refuses to go with Parmeshwara who plans to seduce her under the pretext of providing her a job; she throws a spoonful of hot rasam in the face of a young man who winks at her and a handful of dust into the eyes of a man who tries to molest her. This disappointed man spreads false rumours that she is an adulterous. This rumour cancels her marriage which was about to be settled. This is too heavy a price she has to pay for safeguarding her chastity.

In 'Inquiry into an Offence,' the narrator Kussum had left her husband and come to stay with her parents. Kussum was asked too many questions the society for leaving her husband. Marriage is considered the sole means of a woman's happiness. The housemaid Baby has already fixed marriage of her daughter who is too young. She says: "this is the right age. . . . Children should be married away before they even begin looking around, grasping things. They must have two kids in quick succession. Everything would be alright then" (164).

In 'Bedakata Badukella' the main thrust of the story is on the suicidal death of a young widow, Anju. She believes that woman has no existence without her husband. She finds her life meaningless. She is taught from her infancy that marriage is an everlasting bondage. She commits suicide. Anju says, "Marriage is an illusionary cage that clips the wings of a flying bird and imprisons them." (7) Simon de Beauvoir argues: "Marriage has always been a very different thing for man and for woman. For men it is sexual pleasure, a means to control women and recruit them into their services. . . . For women, it is associated with romantic love and self-sacrifice" (445-46).

In 'Chippu' Yashi has colourful views of marriage just like any other girl. But she is not used to express her feelings. Her mother always nodded her head in approval for everything that the husband said. Parents used to praise Yashi as a very mild and good girl because she does not question. She does not believe in expressing her love by washing husband's clothes or by attracting him through beauty or by satisfying his appetite by cooking. She wishes to love her husband without losing her self-love. No one cared to ask her opinion. She desires to tell all her feelings but her throat dries.

In 'Hakkiladavaru' it is said that Siri is the man of the house. Siri the protagonist possesses virtues of both feminity and masculinity. Her husband leaves her when he faces heavy losses in the hotel business. She is left alone, with her two little children.

Marriage does not provide her any psychological or financial security. She goes back to her maternal home. She works hard for the coconut grove which does not belong to her as she is not a male. Woman has no claim over the property either in her parents' or in her husband's place.

In the story 'Vanimai,' the image of slippers denotes the wish to be 'A New Woman.' The villagers believed that it was only man's privilege to wear slippers. Vanimai is obsessed with a desire to wear slippers. But Narasimha burns her feet for wearing slippers. Thus such a violent punishment is given to women who deviate from the norms of the society. People said to Vani: "why did you incite him . . . is there any chance of surviving if you tease a man? . . . This is what happens if girls desire anything too much!" (197). Vanimai's act of kicking Narasimha, with her feet, even while lying on her deathbed, is a battle against society

Growing-up is a painful process, as one has to oppose the established forces. The unknown path poses new challenges to women. But no one can obstruct her basic need to grow, and to expand her soul. She has her own dreams. Vaidehi makes an attempt to depict the female protagonists who are daring enough to question the patriarchy.

'Gulabi Talkies' explores the lives of men and women disestablished by a couple of unexpected events. The village here has conventional traditions and customs. By the construction of 'Gulabi Talkies' many changes occur in the village. Gulabi Talkies brings about a change in the lives of these women. "The women had to depend on men to go to the tent . . . since the women themselves did not want to go out alone, they did not even imagine how they could be in the street without male company. The men took them to the tent' (2). Women later realize how they are trapped by the male world in spite of their hard work. They are left penniless because their work is considered unproductive. But women do not let this happen for long. They become bold enough to say firmly that they are going to the cinema that evening. As women begin to search for their identity their role begins to change.

In the story 'Babuli,' the shy, hesitant quiet girl Babuli becomes a strong confident person. She contests in municipal elections and works for the upliftment of the downtrodden. She helps the poor and illiterate women in distress. She breaks the barriers of conventions. In 'Ondu Bagila Saddu,' the heroine tries to break away from blind superstitions. She makes an attempt to break free from the rigid conventions by entering the Pooja room and touching the 'Saligrama.' In 'Just a box' Dodamma is mentally strong to take her own decisions and brave enough to get what she wants. She says: "Oh God . . . do I need to proclaim to the entire world, why, where and when? If I desire a box, do I need to justify, and confess?" (95) Chitthi is also a self-loving woman. Despite her old age it is said, "Chitthi prepared elaborate snacks like patrode for herself without complaint! What can u call it, self-love, or passion for life?" (.86)

The wedding house also occupies the space of Vaidehi's stories. The wedding house signifies a whole society with its artificial conventions. In 'Maduve-Hennu-Seere,' Vaidehi portrays the pomp and splendour of a wedding ceremony. Women's state is measured in terms of sarees and jewellery in the wedding house. 'Samaja shastragneya tippanige' expresses people's mentality in the wedding house. We see a girl like Vaarija who is the proud of her parents because she always obeys them and never questions anyone. She does not even express happiness when her marriage gets settled. She is frozen by the upbringing. It also expresses the miserable life of widows. Widows sit in a corner along with other widows as it is considered inauspicious for them to sit near the mandap on such occasions. They are made to shave their heads, wear only red cotton sarees, remove bangles, kumkum and all the jewellery, eat only one meal a day. One widow says that horoscope is very important for marriage. She got married only when her horoscope matched very well. But the irony is that she became widow at fourteenth. We find that all these widows have accepted their life as their fate. These widows support male supremacy because they depend upon it for their survival

In 'Abha,' the space of the story moves outside the home to an outside world. Here we find freedom of expression and freedom of adopting their own lifestyles by women. Here a modern woman Samitha meets a postmodern woman Abha. When "Samitha felt apprehensive about being far away from her hometown," Abha was enjoying her freedom. Abha says: "you know what this thing called marriage is. . . . I think all relationships should stand cancelled and get reshuffled after forty" (31). Abha feels that marital bliss is but an illusion, false and corrupt. Thus Abha is a revolutionary free thinking woman who rejects all traditional values laid down by society. She smokes, drinks, even flirts freely with men. But the story ends with Abha's suicide.

In the story 'Prashne,' the setting is a seminar hall. We see two educated girls Bhuvi and Anu in the seminar. Unlike other women of Vaidehi's stories they express their feelings though socially not acceptable. Bhuvi desires to spend a night with an elderly resource person. She expresses her feelings to him through a letter. The person accepts. But Bhuvi now gets scared. She feels that one can desire many things but has to control herself to live respectfully in society. But to her shock Anu goes with him instead. Here Anu is not a hypocrite and she does not care for what society says. She has already come out of the restricted world.

In 'Shakunthaleyondige Kaleda Aparahna,' space goes back to mythological story of Shakuntala in which Dushyanta forgets Shakuntala because of a curse. But Shakuntala realizes that she was not an important matter for Dushyanta to remember. Shakuntala falls a prey to the advances of the king. Later he promises that he would take her to his palace, but never keeps his word. This betrayal of love causes endless agony for her. Dushyanta's refusal to recognize her raises cold fire in her heart. At last when he comes to take her back she does not go with him. Shakuntala realizes her self-dignity and decides to live alone. Thus Vaidehi depicts the shifting role models and the breakdown of stereotypes that result in the restructuring of the social system

Literature displays the texture of the society. So the writers are bound to create an ideal world. Moreover, the space created by the writer stands as an outlet to channelize the writer's impression of the society. Writer as an artist does not simply copy life but he makes an arrangement out of it to suit his own purposes. Life itself furnishes the writer with material. But he selects, alters and arranges it in his own way so as to create a world of his own. Vaidehi's stories deal with woman's real world, her real experiences. Hence, spaces in her stories are usually kitchen, house, a small village, wedding house and its surroundings where women play a prominent part. Even being strongly rooted in a specific geographical location with a distinct language dialect, Vaidehi's stories achieve a pan-Indian sweep.

## Works Cited

Alegallalli Antharanga, *Sagara*, Karnataka, Akshara Prakashana 2006.

Ashok, T.P., *Vaidehiyavara Kathegalu*, Kundapura Kannada Sangha, 1995.

Simone de Beauvoir, *The Second Sex*, ed. and trans. H.M. Parshley. London: Vintage, 1953.

Vaidehi, *Gulabi Talkies and Other Stories*. Penguin India, 2006.

# Major Trends in English Fiction Produced in Pakistan and Bangladesh

**KRUPALI PAREKH** and **URVASHI KAUSHAL**
**Sardar Vallabhbhai National Institute of Technology, Surat**

English novels from the Indian subcontinent are mostly assumed to be from India as Indian fiction enjoys the central place mostly owing to stalwarts like Salman Rushdie, Vikram Seth, Amitav Ghosh, Arundhati Roy and Aravind Adiga. With Indian English fiction gaining popularity and critical acclaim, the fiction from neighbouring countries like Pakistan and Bangladesh either got overshadowed or engulfed in the blinding light of its recognition. Although these countries are the bifurcated parts of India and share social, political and cultural history with India, they have their own narratives or their version of the story. This paper aims to present a comprehensive survey of the English novels produced since their inception. The list may be limited, yet noteworthy efforts have been made by novelists from both Pakistan and Bangladesh to narrate the stories woven around the social, political and cultural threads of their countries. This paper apart from enlisting the writers and their works also thematically categorises their fiction to bring out the major trends.

## I

In united India and Pakistan, the amount of writing in English by Muslims was little but not negligible. But after being separated from India, Pakistani literature in English started developing and it became an independent body of literature. There were some noticeable writers of pre-partition era (1940).

We can find identity crises in their work and influence of violence during the war for partition. Even after independence, the theme of misery, religious sentiments, tragedy, impact of war, struggle for land, identity crises, violence of partition and the birth of the nation can be seen in their writings.

The theme of partition nourished at the hands of Ahmad Ali, who is considered as a pre-partition Muslim writer. His novel *Twilight in Delhi* (1940) is about India's changing social, political, and cultural climate following colonialism. The novel is set around 1911 to 1919 and portrays the story of the Mughal emperors, their downfall, the rise of British government and the impact of colonialism and imperialism on Muslims. It depicts the picture of old Delhi and its Muslim inhabitants.

Mumtaz Shah Nawaz was a Pakistani woman writer and member of the Muslim League. Her novel *The Heart Divided* is based on a similar theme. The novel gives a record of the partition, colonial experience and riots before the partition. It shows a link between culture and imperialism, issues of changing relationship between Hindus and Muslims, politics of India and colonial ideology. Apart from partition, this novel also portrayed the struggle of the educated and politically active women and its effect on Pakistani women. After her death in 1948, her family published this novel in edited form.

Partition of India and Pakistan and further Pakistan and Bangladesh inspired many creative writers. The novels have been written on the theme of partition in good numbers by the three nations. The theme of partition is not limited to that particular period of time but it continues to intrigue writers even after several decades. This unforgettable historical moment has been captured as horrifying event by novelists like Bapsi Sidhwa in her *The Ice-Candy Man* and Sorayya Khan in her novels *Five Queen's Road* and *Noor*.

Bapsi Sidhwa is a Pakistani Parsi novelist settled in America. Her novel, *The Ice-Candy Man* published in the year

1988, which is also known as *Cracking India,* tells the story of partition. It is about Lahore and deals with the unfortunate partition of India. It presents the turbulent time through the eyes of a young Parsee lady. The novel narrates two major subjects, dislocation and misfortune and was made into a film, "1947: Earth." Commenting on the situation that inspired her to write, in an interview Bapsi Sidhwa remarked, "As a Parsee, I can see things objectively. I see the common people suffering while politicians on either side are having all the fun." (Ahmad)

Sorayya Khan is a Pakistani-European writer. She is the author of *Noor*, *Five Queen's Road,* and *City of Spies* which received the Best International Fiction Book Award in Sharjah International Book Fair, 2015. She was awarded a U.S. Fulbright Research Grant to conduct research in Pakistan and Bangladesh. *Noor* and *Five Queen's Road* which were published in the year 2003 and 2009 respectively, deal with the theme of partition. The novel *Five Queen's Road* represents the period from 1947 to 1980 during which a house in Lahore, Five Queen's Road, undergoes a steady process of decay. Onial Devyani commented, "*Five Queen's Road* stands at the intersection of history and personal memories, a vivid portrait of life as it carries on in all its ordinariness and brutality in the shadow of Partition."

Sorayya Khan's novel *Noor* is based on conflict between East and West Pakistan and the war that eventually created the independent country of Bangladesh. It confronts the trauma caused by war at individual, family and national level. In this regard, Ranasinha commented, "*Noor* dramatizes how individual trauma and guilt seep into the wider collective and complicate family, community and nation." (105)

Kamila Shamsie, a Pakistani-British novelist, was brought up in Karachi and in her teens she moved to London. Her novel *Kartography* published in 2002 is basically a love story. But at the same time it is set around the civil war of 1971. It is about political violence in Pakistan which ruins childhood friendship of major characters, Karim and Rahim. "The novel maps and scrutinizes Karachi's ethnic, classed and gendered spatial politics whilst problematizing rural/ urban binaries." (Ranasinha, 253) This novel was shortlisted for the John Llewellyn Rhys award in the United Kingdom, and won the Patras Bokhari Award from the Academy of Letters in Pakistan.

Mohsin Hamid is a Pakistani writer who lives in U.K. His first novel *Moth Smoke,* published in the year 2000, analyses the theme of partition of the Indian subcontinent in 1947 and the trauma suffered by the people during this violence. The novel won Notable Book of the Year Award in the year 2000, Betty Trask Award in the year 2001 and was shortlisted for Hemingway Foundation/ PEN Award in the same year.

Moni Mohsin grew up in Lahore and later moved to London. *The End of Innocence* was her first novel based on war within Pakistan as well war with India. It shows how friendship between two girls is affected because of war.

The word 'immigration' in general refers to people who leave their homeland and settle in another country either by choice or due to some other reason. The novel written by immigrants tell the stories of their reason for immigration, experience of hostility, search for identity, cultural diversity, sense of rootlessness and much more. The experience of immigration is also found in Pakistani English literature. This painful experience is represented in the work of Nadim Aslam, Mohsin Hamid, Bapsi Sidhwa, Kamila Shamsie, Hanif Kureishi and Zulfikar Ghose. They discuss the moral dilemma and confusion between nativity and alienation. These issues exist not only in the society but also between generations.

Nadeem Aslam is a British Pakistani novelist whose second novel *Map of Lost Lover* was published in 2004. It is set in an unnamed British town where a large community of Pakistani immigrants live. It shows the murder of a pair of lovers and leads to dislocation, exile, alienation dissection of working-class communities of Pakistani immigrants who were the residents of the north of England for the last 40 years. The book took 11 years to finish but won the Kiriyama Prize.

Sidhwa's novel *The Crow Eaters* (1978) concentrates on Parsi families and the Parsi group in the city of Lahore and outlying territories that were incorporated into the newly formed country of Pakistan. *The Crow Eaters* addresses serious cultural and historical issues and gives elements of Parsi culture. At the same time the novel represents cultural hybridity. The central character Faredoon, the head of the Parsi community in Lahore was in favour of the British for the survival of his minority community. The novel shows Parsi's cultural hybridity and peaceful survival.

Sidhwa's *An American Brat* (1993) also shows a glimpse of migration. It is a rich and meaningful document which shows the entire gamut of a diasporic individual's social and psychological conflicts. The novel narrates the story of a young lady who travels through three cultures—her own Parsi culture, her nation Pakistan's Muslim culture and the culture of the United States of America. It falls into two parts: the first part narrates Feroza's story in Pakistan and her reluctance to change, while the second part describes the process of her assimilation in American culture. The novel deals with the change that Feroza experiences in the West and how her viewpoint towards life changes. In an interview to Naila Hussain, Bapsi Sidhwa said that "the book deals with the subject of the 'culture shock' young people from the subcontinent have to contend with when they choose to study abroad. It also delineates the clashes, the divergent cultures generated between the families 'back home' and their transformed and transgressing progeny bravely groping their way in the New World." (Sindh)

Hanif Kureishi's *The Buddha of Suburbia* (1990) analyses the same theme—issue of the identity crisis and the problems of the immigrants in Britain. It portrays young Karim's journey towards self-discovery which ends in restlessness. McLeod elaborates on this point by stating: "to the children of migrants, the 'interior knowledge' of a distant place is unavailable. Thus their reflections about these places in terms of 'home' are often differently constructed." (McLeod) For this novel Kureishi won Whitbread First Novel Award in the year 1990.

The same theme can be found in his second novel *The Black Album* (1995). Shahid, the main protagonist of the novel, lives and grows up in Britain; therefore he adopts the British culture. Shahid then realizes his own culture that he inherited (i.e. the Pakistani culture). He becomes confused over his cultural identity and he decides to search for his true identity.

The theme of cultural dislocation is also present in Zulfikar Ghose's novel, *The Contradictions*, published in 1966, in which an English woman is unable to find her place, either in her homeland (i.e. Pakistan) or in the unfamiliar society of India, where her husband is stationed.

Feminism is another theme which has inspired writers like Kamila Shamsie, Bapsi Sidhwa and Tehmina Durrani. The term 'Feminism' refers to the movement about equal rights and opportunities for men and women. In the novel *The Pakistani Bride*, Sidhwa unfolds the exploitation of women in the patriarchal society: "Women the world over, through the ages, asked to be murdered, raped, exploited, enslaved, to get importunately impregnated, beaten up, bullied and disinherited. It was an immutable law of nature." (Sidhwa)

Bapsi Sidhwa is a postcolonial feminist writer who successfully addressed issues of social and cultural difference and the place of women in the Indian and Pakistani societies. *The Pakistani Bride* (1982) is a heart-touching novel describing the traumatic experiences of a girl named Zaitoon, and her situation before and after marriage in the male dominating Pakistani society. It deals with the oppression of women in the context of psychological and sexual harassment by men in the conservative tribal society. Kamala Edwards observes, "Sidhwa is a feminist and realist. One sees in her women characters the strength of passion, the tenderness of love, and the courage of one's convictions. They struggle to overcome the hurts of time and escape the grip of a fate in whose hands they are often mere puppets." (Raj)

Her novel, *Water: A Novel*, which was also published in 2006, was made into a movie by the same name by the award-winning director Deepa Mehta. "Water" is about the Indian widows of 1930s and how they were forced to live in the widow houses on the banks of Ganga. This novel shows the exploitation of women especially widows by other people and how they are dragged into prostitution.

Mohammed Hanif is a British-Pakistani novelist and journalist. *Our Lady of Alice Bhatti* is his second novel. Published in 2011, it is a highly feminist novel which throws light on the condition of women in the Pakistani society. Alice is a Catholic nurse working at a corrupt Karachi hospital and the novel illustrates in detail all the weird and cruel situations that a woman undergoes in her daily routine. The novel was shortlisted for the Wellcome Trust Book Prize (2012) and the DSC Prize for South Asian Literature (2013).

In *Burnt Shadows* (2009) by Kamila Shamsie, women characters are presented as progressive and realistic. Her protagonist shows stronger moral, ethical and emotional strength than the male characters of the novel. The novel is a story about its central character Hiroko Tania. Her character always believes in moving ahead, the best example being the disaster she faced caused by the dropping of atomic bomb and as she lost her family and love in it. But she gives her life another chance and moves to India, accepts Sajjid's love and marries him but her sufferings seems endless; she has to leave Delhi because of the chaos and anarchy caused by Pakistan-India partition. Later she loses her son Raza and moves to New York. Her character symbolically represents the women victims in the male dominated society. She represents a common woman living under the complete dominance and working under the domination of her husband James Burton. She is gloomy deep inside but fulfils all the duties and responsibilities of a wife very well. She never demands equality and tries to present herself as a happy aristocratic modern wife.

Tehmina Durrani is a Pakistani novelist who fought for women's rights. *My Feudal Lord,* her controversial book, provided the world a great insight into the defenceless position of women stuck in the complex web of Pakistani society. It is as riveting as it is scandalous and was translated into 39 languages. Pakistani writers have also portrayed socio-political events in their novels. It presents a realistic scenario of society and politics through their fictional characters.

The novel *In the City by the Sea* by Kamila Shamsie, published in 1998, is set in one of the cities in Pakistan which is in the middle of a political struggle. The novel is based on the events in the country under the dictatorial military rule, and this political unrest affects many people of Pakistan. She unfolds the life of a leader of opposition through the character of Salman Mamu and portrays the political scenario of Pakistan through the depiction of its major city—Karachi. We can feel the problems of Karachi through the eyes of the 11 year old protagonist Hasan. The condition of Salman Mamu reminds us of those politicians or public leaders who were punished by the ruling party just because they rebelled against the exploitation of malicious politicians. *The City by the Sea* is not just an epic managing with large-scale events, but an account of a boy's adoration for his family, and the role imagination plays in the mind of a child.

Shamsie's novel *Broken Verses* (2005) narrates the dictatorship of politicians: Zulfikar Ali Bhutto and Zia ul-Haq. The daughter of Aasmani-Samina was beaten by the forces of Zia ul-Haq whose aim was to 'send violent tremors down the spine of women's movement.' The policy of these political leaders was to divide the nation on the basis of religious and ethical borderline. The novel represents the 1970s and 80s of Pakistan.

Zulfikar Ghose's *The Murder of Aziz Khan* (1967) presents Pakistani society in its earliest years. Ghose compares Aziz Khan, a symbol of old and traditional values, with the Shah Brothers, who misuse the assets and individuals of the new nation for their personal gain. The complex story gradually uncovers the emotions of its characters and describes the misery of Aziz Khan.

Mohammed Hanif's *A Case of Exploding Mangoes* published in 2008 is about the plane crash that executed General Muhammad Zia ul-Haq, one of the Presidents of Pakistan. The book won the Best First Book Award in 2009 in the Commonwealth Book Prize. It was also shortlisted for the Guardian First Book Award. *The Guardian* depicted the novel as 'woven in a language as explosive as the mangoes themselves, is wickedly cynical and reveals layers of outrageous—and plausible—corruption.' (*The Guardian*, New Delhi)

Fatima Bhutto's debut novel *The Shadow of Crescent Moon* (2013), set during the American invasion of Afghanistan, depicts how a small tribal town, Mir Ali in Pakistan (located near Afghan border) is affected due to this. The novel begins and ends on one rain swept-Friday morning and talks about five young people who are pushed to make terrible choices during a single day. As the events of this single morning unfold a family and the country undergoes a drastic change.

There are some writers who have dealt with other themes and represent different culture, land, scenario, characters etc. Ahmed Ali's novel, *Ocean of Night* published in 1964, is about the background of Lucknow which was the centre of Indo-Muslim culture. His *Rats and Diplomats*, published in 1995, is a satiric novel about a diplomatic mission of an imaginary country 'Bachusan.'

Unhappy married life and extra-marital affairs have been discussed in Hanif Kureishi's *Intimacy* (1998). The protagonist of the novel lives in London and is very unhappy with his married life and wishes to leave the family. It shows a contradiction between sexual and intellectual desires of the protagonist. His other novel *Gabriel's Gift* published on 2001 is the tale of a protagonist who wants to be a filmmaker. It is about meditation on failure, talent, the power of imagination, and portrays the generation who only thinks about growing up. *Something to Tell You*, published in 2008, is based on emptiness, unsuccessful married life, unsatisfied desire of Jamal, the middle-aged protagonist.

Bina Shah's first novel *Where They Dream in Blue* published in 2001, depicts the journey of a young boy who decides to shift to the new land, Karachi from United States to explore the city where his parents were born and lived. *The 786 Cyber Cafe* (2004), is about a young Pakistani man's virtual worlds of internet sex and online faith. Her novel *Slum Child* (2010) characterises a poor girl and the journey of her miserable life. The novel is said to be based on Marxist theory. Her *A Season for Martyrs* (2014) is about last three months of Benazir Bhutto's life.

## II

Bangladeshi novels in English emerged after the partition of East and West Pakistan. The East Pakistan has become Bangladesh which emerged as an independent nation in the year 1971. The war between East Pakistan and West Pakistan that lasted for nine months is known as the Bangladesh liberation war. One of the key reasons of this partition was the cultural differences; the people of East Pakistan followed the Bengali culture but the West Pakistan tried to impose their Islamic culture on East Pakistan. Besides, East Pakistan was completely neglected in the spheres of politics, economics, development and all other needs of the nation which led to the war.

As Bangladesh became an independent nation in the year 1971, the literature of the nation is limited. The writers and their writings are not many as compared to other South Asian countries. There are few but prominent writers of Bangladesh who contributed to English Fiction and whose writing skills are praised by many critics. Many of them have immigrated and have emerged as Bangladeshi Diaspora writers. Monica Ali, Tahmima Anam, Neamat Imam K., Anis Ahmed etc. are the prominent writers. These writers discovered many themes in their writings with Bangladesh as a background. Some of them are enlisted below.

*Brick Lane* (2003) by Monica Ali is based on the themes of cultural alienation, immigrant experience and personal growth in the new land. It narrates the story of Nazneen, who comes to England from Bangladesh at the age of 18, after an arranged marriage to Chanu. Nazneen not only has to learn to live with Chanu, but she has to survive in a completely new culture as well. She is always an outsider, an immigrant in a foreign land, and her Bangladeshi roots keep her in a subservient role in her married life and family. When she arrived in the new land she could barely speak two words in English. Nazneen struggles to make a life for herself within her traditional marriage and the immigrant community. Sukhdev Sandhu's review of *Brick Lane* in *The London Review of Books* traces some part of the history of this exclusion, noting that from as early as the eighteenth century the area has been "a home for those who have been pushed out of their homes." (Hiddleston) It was made into a film in 2007 by the same name. The novel received encouraging reviews by critics in the U.K. and the U.S and was shortlisted for the Man Booker Prize.

Another novel which shares the same theme as *Brick Lane* is *Life, Love and Assimilation* by Kia Abdulla published in 2006. It is based on a Bangladeshi girl's life in the East; her struggle to live in London and adopt its social norms, as her parents belong to Bangladesh. The novel discusses issues such as preference of son, arranged marriage and women having little freedom. The major concept of the novel is the problems different generations have to face as immigrants. These people try to blend fully in both the cultures and yet they are considered outsiders in London and never remain fully Bangladeshi. Apart from this, the novel also depicts the issues of drug addiction, gender inequality, and arranged marriage.

*French Lover* (2001) by Taslima Nasrin shares the same theme. The novel is about a Bengali woman, Nilanjana from Kolkata who moves to Paris after her arranged marriage to Kishanlal. She wanted to explore France's history and wanted to live her life on her own terms. But her husband wants her to be a housewife. As a result she starts to feel like a caged animal, stifled within its friendless confines. She is unable to have her own identity in the new land and she desperately longs to change her status. Finally she leaves her husband and starts searching for her own identity. The novel is based on the struggle for identity in this hostile world. The novel discusses the issue of male dominance, failure in love, search for love, lesbian relationship etc.

Tahmima Anam's *The Bones Grace* (2016) is about the love life of the protagonist Zubaida. But at the same time it is about belonging, migration, tragedy, survival, and the mysteries of origins, in short her search for self. She is caught between countries, cultures and two men: Rashid, the Bangladeshi childhood sweetheart and Elijah, the American drifter. "This book is fundamentally about a woman trying to win back the love of her life. When I realized that it really helped to shape the whole thing." (Kidd) And to choose between these two men is the central idea of the plot.

*The Black Coat* (2013), a novel by Neamat Imam, is a political satire. It is a tale of liberation of Bangladesh in 1971, after a bloody struggle. Thousands were pouring into Dhaka from everywhere, looking for security, and to fulfill primary requirements like food and shelter. Amongst them is Nur Hussain, an uneducated young fellow from a remote village. He turns up as a writer at Khaleque Biswas's doorstep, looking for a job. With the blessings of the political foundation, he begins to earn good amount of money and starts to help the poor people of the city. But at the same time politics turns violent and nation suffers from the serious problems of starvation in the year 1974. With flair to pen a realistic picture of his milieu Imam writes, "The person who goes against the government is not an enemy of the people. Those who accept their government's limitations in silence are the real enemies."

Kazi Anis Ahmed's *The World in My Hand* (2013) is also a satiric novel and talks about the similar theme like *The Black Coat*. Bangladesh was dominated by two parties; The Patriotic Party of Pandua and the Social Democratic Party, the endless feud of these two leaders continued for a long period of time. The novel shows the suffering of a group of companions—Hissam, Kaiser and Natasha—who struggle to hold together their profoundly polarized individual lives against the backdrop of a grand political partition. Hissam is a deputy news manager, who was ready to leave the country as the national crisis grew worse. Kaiser was a real estate tycoon and Natasha, his wife, was involved in social activities with an NGO, and was also Hissam's "dearest." The novel shows how their lives were affected due to the situations and conditions of contemporary Bangladesh.

*In the Light of What We Know* (2014) by Zia Haider Rahman is set during the war of Afghanistan and illustrates the suffering of common people and the financial crises during this war. The narrator is an unnamed Pakistani-American banker whose career collapses and marriage becomes unstable, the novel further explores the questions of belongingness, love and war.

Tahmima Anam's first novel *A Golden Age* (2007) is a novel about war for independence of Bangladesh. It is the story of the protagonist Rehana Haque, a widow who loses the custody of her children when the novel opens and after getting their custody, the novel records her struggle to protect them. At the same time it shows Bangladesh liberation war and how this family suffers due to it as both her children were involved in the war. Anam personally met people and took interviews, who had experienced the war. In one of her interviews she said, "I thought I would write a sort of epic, a very muscular narrative that had battle scenes and political rallies and all the sorts of big moments that you see in war novels. But actually, when I sat down to write, I ended up really thinking about what it was like for ordinary people to survive that war." (Neary) *The Guardian* described *A Golden Age* as a "stunning debut." The novel was shortlisted for the Guardian First Book Award in the year 2007. It was awarded the prize for Best First Book in the Commonwealth Writers' Prize in 2008.

Tahmima Anam's novel *The Good Muslim* (2011) is a sequel to her novel *A Golden Age* and focuses on the cruel impact of the Bangladesh liberation war. *The Good Muslim* continues the story of the characters of *The Golden Age*, Maya and Sohail who were separated during the war, and meet after a long time. This separation made a lot of changes in their perspective. Sohail became a religious leader whereas Maya tried to pursue her revolutionary ideals. The conflict between brother and sister and their different ideals is the main crux of the novel. It is about cruelty of war and how people's lives are affected by it. Speaking about her writing Anam remarked in an interview, 'I did lots of research for my first book which carried over to the second. I prefer to ask people who were there about their experiences.' (You Tube)

*Lajja* (1993), originally written in Bengali and later translated into English, is a novel by Taslima Nasrin. It is about communal riots that erupted in Bangladesh because of the demolition of Babri Masjid. The centre of this novel is Dutta Family (Sudhamoy, Kironmoyee, and their two children, Suranjan and Maya) who faced the communal hatred as they belonged to the small Hindu community that was terrorized by Muslims. During these riots many of their friends immigrate to India but they refuse to leave their country.

Apart from the above, there are few novels which have been written on different themes like Monica Ali's *In the Kitchen* (2009) which represents the busy kitchen of a restaurant in central London, where Gabriel Lightfoot, her main character, is an executive chef. Characters remind us that no one will live permanently on this earth. Gabriel's kitchen represents a variety of immigrants in Britain. Every corner of the earth is represented here, Hispanic, Asian, African, Baltic and places between this. In the novel characters argue about the complex issues of race, culture and progress.

*Alentejo Blue* (2006) by Monica Ali is a novel set in a Portuguese village. It is a story of displacement and modernism which is told by the locals and people who experience such a problem. The characters are sympathetic. An old worker, a fat café-owner, a Portuguese young lady, a disappointed English tourist, a disappointed English writer—all these stock characters run through the beautiful town with its vivid colours. The novel shows deeper understanding of the characters, their dreams, desires and disappointments.

*Child's Play* (2009) by Kia Abdulla is a suspense thriller with central character Allegra Ashe, a young lady who is manipulated into joining a mysterious government unit that targets pedophiles. It's disturbing in parts, touching in others as it deals with the sensitive issue of child abuse.

With many different characters, the novel *Days of Our Wives* (2013) by Salman Jones also shows the journey of different characters like the above-mentioned novel. It investigates the world of characters that include a prostitute, a *hajj* administrator, a killer, a cannabis farmer and a gay pilot. It captures around more than 10 years and depicts the expectations, dreams and struggles of the Bengali protagonists; it also shows her adventurous journey to discover love, loss and betrayal.

To conclude, we can say that Pakistan and Bangladesh have produced noteworthy fiction in English that confronts the issues of their culture and society and sometimes of the sub-continent in general. Although limited but significant narratives from these former parts of India voice their problems and perceptions on various issues like war, women, violence, immigration, politics and corruption. A close reading of these texts can open myriad opportunities for debate, discussion, deliberation and analysis.

## Works Cited

Ahmad, Nadia. "Cracking India: Cultural and Religious Representation in Indo-Anglian Literature," *Queen: A Journal of Rhetoric and Power* (n.d.), Volume 21.

Chambers Claire, Herbert. *Imagining Muslims in South Asia and the Diaspora: Secularism, Religion, Representations*, Routledge, 2015.

Finney, Brian. *English Fiction since 1984: Narrating a Nati*on, Palgrave Macmillan UK, 2006.

Hiddleston, Jane. "Shapes and Shadows: (Un)veiling the Immigrant in Monica Ali's *Brick Lane*," *The Journal of Commonwealth Literature* (2014): 57-72.

Imam, Neamat. *The Black Coat*, UK: Penguin, 2013.

Kidd, James. "Bangladeshi Novelist Tahmima Anam Discusses Cultural Identity and Her Latest Novel *The Bones of Grace*," *The National,* 1 June 2016.

Mahadevan-Dasgupta, Uma. Review of Sorayya Khan's *Noor*, *India Today,* 12 April 2004.

McLeod, John. *Beginning Postcolonialism*, Manchester: Manchester University Press, 2000.

Neary, Lynn. "At Home, at War: Tahmima Anam's *Golden Age*," *NPR Books*, 11 Jan. 2008.

Onial, Devyani. "Subcontinental Shifts," *The Indian Express*, 7 Nov. 2009.

Raj, S. Anandh. "Feminism in Bapsi Sidhwa's *Ice-Candy Man*," *Pune Research: An International Journal in English* (2016).

Ranasinha, Ruvani. *Contemporary Diasporic South Asian Women's Fiction*, London: Palgrave Macmillan, 2016.

Redford, Rachel. "A Case of Exploding Mangoes," *The Guardian,* 26 Jan. 2009

Sidhwa, Bapsi. *The Pakistani Bride*, Minneapolis: Milkweed, 2008, p. 227.

Sindh, Randhir Pratap. "Bapsi Sidhwa," New Delhi: Ivy, 2005, p. 65.

# Patriarchy Re-Evaluated: Invisible Men in Tehmina Durrani's *Blasphemy* and *My Feudal Lord*

**GEETANJALI RATHORE**
**Rohru, Himachal Pradesh**

Patriarchy is one of the most essential aspects, which should be studied at length, to be able to lucidly comprehend gender studies in its entirety. Discourses on patriarchy delineate patriarchy to be fundamentally the power of male head over the family, which constitutes his sons and wife. According to *Oxford English Dictionary*, Patriarchy is a "form of social organization in which the father or the oldest male is the head of the family and descent and relationships are reckoned through the male line; Government or rule by man or men." This concept persistently registers its presence in the scholarly contributions due to the conspicuous absence of an egalitarian arrangement in man-woman relationship. Patriarchy as a matter of fact holds the potential to dehumanize the other half of history. Also patriarchy is no more only the rule of the father it has acquired new connotations and dimensions over the decades. The general meaning of the male head has long been defunct now. Patriarchy is operating not only at personal level but also at political levels; there is a serious interaction between the private matters and different power structures that co-exist in the society. Personal has now transmuted into political." Therefore this state of affairs is entitled to a constant renewed and vigorous analysis at regular intervals; and the notion of patriarchy being a redundant theory can safely be put to rest.

Varied views about the concept of patriarchy are expressed by traditionalists, radical feminists, Marxist feminists and in Sylvia Walby's Dual System Theory. There is no uniform consensus as to what is patriarchy? Prior to scrutinizing gender portrayal in the selected novels for this paper, it becomes essential to analyze the concept of patriarchy through the above-mentioned approaches.

Traditionalists and renowned scholars like Aristotle believe that a woman is nothing but a 'mutilated' male. Radical feminists believe family to be the site of male domination. According to them the body of a female is the pivot which provides a stronghold to the concept of patriarchy.

Radical feminists have been criticized for their approach which revolves around male domination over females. They are also sometimes termed as 'man haters.' But this theory also exudes the idea of males as the enemies of women and also the absence of universality is noticeably visible in this concept. Sylvia Walby's critical theory of Dual System contends the misappropriation of the bodies and labour of women precipitates the suppressed status of women and powerful status of males. Sylvia Walby believed patriarchy to be interlocked with feminism. Marxist feminists on the other hand focused on the labor power of women as to how and where it was employed; what impact it had on the status of women as individuals.

Modern thinkers like Simone de Beauvoir, Firestone and Sylvia Walby conformed to the above-stated views whereas postmodern thinkers like Carole Pateman are of the view that gender discrimination has been checked at the political level but it continues to thrive at the domestic level.

At various levels these theories have been criticized for their ahistoric analysis, biologism, and universalism and they also face the stance of being essentialist. Radical feminism explores the gender relationships at the level of men and women, whereas dual system theory and Marxists explore the possibility of exploitations through class and capitalism.

The assumptions that underlie the structure of human society are so ancient and buried that our way of life appears to be 'natural,' crucial and as inevitable as wind or gravity. In order to gain a complete insight into impact of patriarchy on gender relations this paper endeavours to study different set of patriarchal relations not from men and women perspective but the impact that patriarchy causes on men. A complete focus only on the suppression of women will render a sexist approach to this paper and also to the society. In this case the entire rationale of writing this paper would be defeated. Many consider patriarchy to be an outdated concept but observation and continuous contributions by scholars confirm that it is acquiring new dimensions at an immensely rapid speed. Studying patriarchy from the angle of gender aspect expands the arena under which this concept can be seen. It brings to light the other agencies concerned in perpetuating patriarchy. The writer has precisely brought to the fore the multi layers of power structures that are embedded within the patriarchal structures.

This aspect deserves notice, wherein we can perceive how women act as an agency in perpetuating patriarchy. Women also assist men in carrying out their whims and fancies against other women in order to evict themselves from the vicious influences of patriarchy and have access to the power and control which men possess. This is due to the lack of confidence to raise voices against men and be independent. Also this power structure and construct called patriarchy has sturdily percolated into the belief system of women and controls their minds. On the other hand there are many women who teach their daughters norms of patriarchy. We are very much aware of the marginalizing of women by men in every way. They execute it on social, economic, physical, mental, emotional and even reproduction level. Elements like culture are held as pivots which decide the seemingly tangible stance of gender relations. Westwood and Bhachu write: "Patriarchal relations are neither monolithic nor static, but contexted by cultural elements in which they interact."

Not only women but also younger or non-dominating men are subjected to subordination by the patriarch or the head of the family. In this situation we see that males in their early age learn to be patriarchs through a regime which is internalized by them over a long period. We can also see that males have equally less probability to formulate a mindset of their individual preference; since they are taught at a young age about what is 'natural' to a man, we scarcely realize that in bringing up boys 'naturally,' a disastrous mass production of patriarchs is on the way. Phrases like 'men do not cry,' 'men do not play with dolls or teddy bears' or 'this is not manly' are nothing but undetectable pressures of patriarchy on men as well. Amusingly these clichés have translated into norms and rules of different societies to an extent and continue to thrive in the society as 'natural.' In the process the point is missed that males are also gendered through systems like performative theory. Men also perform their genders just as women do. Susan Kingsley in her paper "Gender: what is it? Who has it?" aptly remarks: "We tend not to see men as 'gendered' creatures but as the standard against which the inadequacies or insufficiencies of women are displayed." (3)

Minute observations substantiate that relationship between genders is that of power, inequality, subordination, oppression, and difference. Gender relations should be studied distinct of liberal, radical, Marxist or dual system theory. They should be studied from the angle of power which seeks to subordinate and suppress. The power to be able to suppress and control women grants the male 'his superiority' and his masculinity. That is why women act an agency for patriarchy since it grants them an egalitarian status with men, which is power in other terms. Connell in his book says: 'Power operating through institutions, power in the form of oppression of one group by another is an important part of the structure of gender.'

The above-mentioned thought-provoking concerns are ingrained in the novels of Tehmina Durrani. She has expertly focused on varied discrepancies in patriarchal order which jeopardize and victimize the lives of not only women but also men. She expands on feudalism in her novel *My Feudal Lord* and creation of a religious shrine and misinterpretation of Quran for convenience in her novel *Blasphemy*. These two novels are thriving with the instances where we see gender oppression and patriarchy being the agency of suppression of either of the sex.

Interestingly patriarchy can be studied not only from the totally other angle which can be evaluation of the effects of patriarchy on men. If aptly appropriated, most likely all men live under the invisible shadow of patriarchy. Unequal gender relations are no more a woman and man only issues. There are men who think from the women perspective also. Society has not only set up a how to be a woman manual but also a manual which instructs on how to be a man. There are ample examples in the chosen novels which shows how men who have the power to take decisions dominate the younger men who are dependent on them financially or of a softer frame of mind. If Simone de Beauvoir says, "Women are not born, they are made"; analogous to this statement it can also be said that patriarchs are not born they are made. Connell in his *Question of Gender* opines: "Being a man or a woman is not a fixed state. It is a becoming, a condition actively under construction. The pioneering French feminist Simone de Beauvoir put this in a classic phrase: 'one is not born, but rather becomes a woman.' Though the positions of women and men are not simply parallel, the principle is also true for men. One is not born masculine, but acquires and enacts masculinity and so becomes a man." (4)

The ways of becoming a man coincides with R.W. Connell's theory of Male hegemony which concentrates on the socially most acceptable male personality. The theory brings to the fore the culturally and socially most idealized ways of being a man. The theory of patriarchy propagates the masculinity which glorifies and deglorifies hegemonic male. Tehmina Durrani's novels deal with the hegemonic male who confuses rudeness with strength and violence with power. One gap that appears in the issue is that these males are themselves tortured and are framed the way they are in the image of the hegemonic male. In Tehmina's novel *Blasphemy* Heer's mother treats her son in a very despicable manner. She expects him to bring home money, take the responsibility of his sisters, study and earn a high office. Worth-noting is that she does not expect anything of her daughters, she expects them to get good matches and marry off in well off households. After their marriages in the so-called well off households she taunts her son that she bore three sons and one daughter. She maims her son a daughter and vice versa because the daughters are not financially dependent on her but the son is not earning much. A son gains acceptance when he earns and takes responsibility of the finances of the family. Why this expectation is not made of girls and women?

Pir Sain excessively and lovingly involves with street dogs. His father locks him up with the many puppies for several days without food. Such cruel behaviour from men in power crushes even the slightest flicker for emotion and affection in younger men. The passion of subduing any soft emotion continues in the lineage and Pir Sain kills his own younger son because he finds his son unable to connect with him. After Pir Sain's death, his elder son mistreats his mother but when she leaves the house on death bed he bids farewell to her with tears in his eyes. He knows that he has been unjust to his mother although she was not wrong he half knows that his mother is alive but allows her body to be taken because he knows that he had to identify with his cruel uncles otherwise he will be treated as an outcast and may be killed like his brothers. Heer's brother cries for her, remains sad and understands her pain and wants to set her free from the vicious circle but is unaware of the vicious circle of his own life where he is unacceptable to his own mother.

On the other hand in Tehmina Durrani's *My Feudal Lord* Mustafa Khar's behaviour towards his servant is ridiculous. He beats him for every small thing like not setting the breakfast table on time; men also visibly reel under the pressures of patriarchy. Tehmina cheats her first husband Anees cruelly although it was a love marriage. A mere confession cannot absolve her of the deed. Not only men divorce women there are also women who cheat and leave their husbands without any reason. Also Mustafa cheats Anees and marries his wife Tehmina. In his capacity as a Governor he sends him on various fictitiously confidential missions. He does all this in order to be able to enjoy with his wife Tehmina and consequently marry her. Tehmina's father comes across as a very silent and docile person whereas her mother comes forth as a strong-headed and strong-willed woman. Her father visibly does not take any important decisions in the family. In the end he takes one final decision and marries another woman.

Tehmina's mother on the other hand denies any emotional support to Tehmina during her abusive marriage to Mustafa Khar. After Tehmina's strong-headed mother and docile father, her soft-hearted brother is seen who supports her in every situation of her life. Therefore to uphold the notion of only the males as abusive and heartless would be a sexist approach. The approach should be all-inclusive and not only from the angle of men or women. Although gender is an umbrella term but mostly women get priority in the critical analysis.

The above illustrations point out that not only women but men also suffer in the patriarchal set-ups. Not only men expect a particular standard to be met by a male but also women expect a man to be 'manly' and specifically the 'hegemonic male.' Gendered relation equation is unequal not only between man and woman but also between a man and man. This new and added dimension requires a thoroughly minute observation which will help in bringing out the mores of patriarchal and gender relations.

This paper does not deny the sufferings of the women in the novels of Tehmina Durrani but also tries to enlighten on the condition of men in these novels. Their position is almost lurking, invisible and unaddressed. On the other hand it is visible in many literary works that women are abused and live a maltreated life but the cause of why men treat women in such a way is still left unaddressed. The above discussed causes bring about the brutally mutilated personalities of males. Male chauvinism is not only a burden for the society but also for the male carrying it. We as a society have not left any option open for men. There is a totally new discourse which is under way. This new discourse needs to be addressed and made defunct by probing patriarchy from all angles.

## Works Cited

Butler, Judith. *Gender Trouble*: *Feminism and the Subversion of Identity*. New York: Routledge, 1990.

Connell, R.W. *Masculinities*, Cambridge, UK: Polity Press, 1993.

Durrani, Tehmina. *My Feudal Lord*. New Delhi: Penguin, 1994.

Durrani, Tehmina. *Blasphemy*. New Delhi: Penguin, 1998.

Kent, Susan K. *Gender and History*. Basingstoke: Palgrave Macmillan, 2012.

# A Study of Identity, Partition, Religion and Diaspora in Bapsi Sidhwa's *Ice-Candy Man*

**SHRIDHARA C.R.**
**Government First Grade College, Nonavinakere, Tumkur**

The times of conflict always bring out the best in a few and the worst in most of the people in a society. The bonds which connect diverse groups together come under extreme strain resulting in a shift in identities. The partition of India in 1947 is such a terrible phenomenon which changed the lives of millions forever. This man-made political disaster resulted in the massacre of around five million people, the abduction of more than one million women and the dislocation of more than a billion.

The diaspora or a migrated community, especially a minority, faces a dilemma during unrest. They prefer either to be invisible or with the winning side. When nation states form among the religious lines such as Pakistan, their identity has to be as less assertive as possible to not be looked as a threat.

Partition of India saw violence in its utmost ugliness, especially on women. They were abducted, mutilated and killed. The survivors were ostracized by their families and society. Violence and retaliation has left numerous unhealed scars on India and Pakistan. It also shaped the identities of three countries in South Asia. According to Ayesha Jalal, a Pakistani historian, partition is "a defining moment that is neither beginning, nor end. Partition continues to influence how the peoples and states of postcolonial South Asia envisage their past, present and future."

*Ice-Candy Man* by Bapsi Sidhwa gives a fictional account of partition narrated by an adolescent girl. The novel was first published in 1988. It is set in the 1940s when the history of India took a bloody turn which unleashed the utmost barbarity of humankind. The novel looks at the unpredictability of human behaviour, deflation in values and the destruction of sensibilities in a society during partition.

The narrator in the novel is Lenny. She is triply marginalized by being a Parsee, a girl and a handicapped one at that. The reader can be almost deceived that the narrator is really an adolescent girl. However she often shifts to a higher tone and provides her opinions and comments. We can assume that the adult Lenny is reliving her past in order to make sense of the events that took place. The story is not what an eight-year-old girl sees; it is what she remembers as an adult. As we know, memory can deceive us. To decide whether the narrator deliberately tries to prove that her story is 'true' is up to the reader.

Parsees are a minority in India. They fled Persia to escape the persecution by aggressive Islam conquerors. Industrious and intelligent, they prospered in the subcontinent but held on to their religious identity. Lenny, even though a sceptic in the matters of faith, experiences a kind of peacefulness while kneeling before the holy fire. She believes in God and prays for the well-being of everyone. In times of conflict, Parsees choose the winning side. During the freedom struggle, most of the Parsees supported the British. Since they are a minority, they prefer security instead of turmoil. In the novel, people like Col. Bharucha blame the British government in casual talking, but as a community, they favour the British. In the community meeting, which is described with a touch of humour by Sidhwa, Parsees wholeheartedly pray for the British. When the war is over, they are happy that the 'defector' Bose did not win. They even hold a 'Jashan' to celebrate the victory of the British.

The novel is a bildungsroman of sorts. Lenny goes through numerous experiences which make a great impression on her psyche and transforms her personality. In the presence of Ayah and her admirers she learns about strange passions which hover around men and women. Ayah is like a lady bird. Her admirers woo her in their different ways. This world of desire and passion awakens something in Lenny. She becomes aware of different dimensions of human relationships: "My nose inhales the fragrance of earth and grass and the other fragrance that distils insights" (19). In her plays and quarrels with her cousin. Lenny becomes more and more aware of her identity as a woman. Her curiosity about men increases. "I look about me with new eyes. The world is athrob with men" (219). This world of passions and desires is thrilling and attractive to her. The lion in the zoo is a symbol for animalistic passions inside people. The caged passions of her admirers just prowl around Ayah. But she tames them as a master. However, partition fills the veins of society with insanity. Once the riots start, the passions are unleashed and they show their barbaric side. The bonds of trust, friendship and sympathy are broken. Ayah's admirers become her violators. Even a father-figure like Imam Din becomes one of them.

The changes at the national level affect Lenny's small world. The conversations between her adult friends change gradually from a friendly talk to argument and finally to the level of deep hatred. Lenny watches helplessly as people cease to be individuals and become Hindus, Muslims and Sikhs. They become one with faceless and mindless mobs.

Lenny witnesses religious identities getting more and more aggressive as the days go by. Politics and religion get prominence in their talks. In the beginning, Ayah succeeds in distracting them but slowly the friendly chats give way to heated arguments. Communities get very conscious about their identities in the testing times. Asserting one's own identity is a psychological response of stronger communities in the times of conflict. Ice-candy man's comments on Sikhs, that they are puppets in the hands of Hindus, receive anger from Sher Singh. Finally when Ice-candy man half-confesses half-boasts that he has killed Hindus and burnt their homes, the thin string of friendship that holds the group breaks down. It is evident in the words of the Gardener who finds it hard to believe people he called brothers are ready to kill him now. Lenny senses the animosity growing. Her nightmares about the lion and the siren symbolize the terrible events to follow.

The realization about religious differences comes very suddenly to Lenny. "One day everybody is themselves—and the next day they are Hindu, Muslim, Sikh, Christian. People shrink, dwindling into symbols" (93). Religious communities turn to their symbols more vigorously when they are threatened. It results in the othering of the 'enemy.' Ayah's worships, Imam Din and Yousuf's prayers which they neglected before are examples of that. However untouchables like Hari, Machoo and Papoo get confused. Hari tries to grow his bodhi to assert his Hindu identity but when the threat to his life is imminent, he converts to Islam. Another untouchable family becomes Christian. The difference between the dominant and the marginal in a society during partition is striking. While the former clings to his/ her identity strongly, the latter is ready to change in order to survive.

The above point brings another aspect of partition to light. In the novel, the narrator recognizes characters wearing the mask of religion in order to profit from the situation. In Lahore, the Hindu moneylenders are looted and in Punjab the Muslim and Hindu landholders are evicted. Ice-candy man turns into a monster because of his jealousy of the masseur and to avenge the death of his family. The reaction of a Hindu priest when the shadows of Yousuf and Lenny cross him plants a deep hatred in Yousuf. Ice-candy man points out at different social and personal sins coming together to culminate in a tragedy.

The Ice-candy man is a symbol of the age. The readers do not know who he really is. His identity is fluid, ever-changing. He is a man of all seasons, changing with the times. He brings the news of the outside world to Ayah. Even though an admirer, his approach to Ayah is a little perverse and aggressive. Ironically, he uses the name of religion and nation to defend his crimes.

Major political events and figures of the time are seen as from a telescope. Lenny's world is very small. She perceives changes through the changes in her friends. This makes her narration a history from the point of view of a subaltern. However, the narration is not completely devoid of political colour. Gandhi is seen as a manipulator who led the country into a tragedy: "Gandhi visits Lahore, I'm surprised he exists. I almost thought he was a mythic figure" (85). The distance between Lenny's world and the outside world is very big. However the narrator points a finger of accusation towards Gandhi. She holds him responsible for the massacres that were to follow. In the eyes of the narrator Nehru is a charming politician who is favoured by the British while Jinnah is a straightforward lawyer-turned-statesman who somewhere could not compete with Nehru in pleasing them.

The birth of a new nation and the identity as its citizen cannot be fully comprehended by Lenny. She is struck by the sudden shift in her identity, thus changing her existence. To a child who can only understand physical changes, this seems strange. "I'm a Pakistani, in a snap, just like that." She struggles to imagine the division of a country. "Can one break a country? And what happens if they break it where our house is? Or crack it further upon Warris road? How will I ever get to godmother's then?" (92). The absurdity of the cruel fate is sounded in the innocent question of villagers of Pir Pindo. When the Gorkha soldiers come to evict them, one of the villagers asks: "what? Is Pakistan already there?"

Despite the gloom that envelops on the story, a small ray of hope shines in Lenny's world because of some women in Parsee community. They help the victims of partition and look for Ayah everywhere. The sympathy and bondage among women is emphasized in their portrayal. The women in *Ice-Candy Man* are not just victims. Despite the unthinkable cruelty inflicted upon them, they spring back and try hard to heal the wounds of the time.

*Ice-Candy Man* is the saga of sufferings seen by an adolescent. The ugly side of religious and geographical identities is revealed here. It is also about the transformation in the personality of Lenny who gets educated about the innermost desires and passions. She also becomes aware of the brutal instincts which lurk behind every common person. The novel brings forth the play of conflicting identities in the terrible phenomenon called partition. It points out at social differences, prejudices, economic interests, personal grudges, political and religious identities all coming together in the time of partition to fulfil their own ends through violence. The novel also looks at human values getting destroyed in the turmoil, but retains hope in the deeds of a few sensible people.

## Bibliography

Sidhwa, Bapsi. *Ice-Candy Man*. New Delhi: Penguin, 1989.

https;//archive.org/stream/ParsisInIndiaAndTheDiaspora/John_Hinnels_Parsis_In_India_And_The_Diaspora

Jalal, Ayesha. *The Pity of Partition: Manto's Life, Time, Works across the India Divide*: Princeton: Princeton University Press, 2013.

Gaur, Rashmi, ed. *Bapsi Sidhwa's* Ice-Candy Man*: A Reader's Companion*. New Delhi: Prestige, 2004.

# Gender Stereotypes and Feminist Strokes: Negotiating the Spaces in Mills and Boon

**REEMA CHAKRABARTI**
**Junior Research Fellow, Indian School of Mines, Dhanbad**

Founded by Gerald Rusgrove Mill and Charles Boon in the year 1908, the harlequin enterprise was a general publishing house that brought out all sorts of books from travel guides to arts and craft. The first book however, was a romance novel named *Arrows from the Dark* by Sophie Cole. It was received with great success and simultaneously, more than thousand manuscripts landed in the office of Mills and Boon. As a consequence, it became easier for Charles Boon to realize that the future of company's progress rested in the demands of the fairer sex. More than hundred years have passed since its establishment, and the circulation of these books have expanded at a global level. Every month, a series of books are published under various imprints whose contents range from innocent love to explicit description of sexual activities. (An imprint of a publisher is a trade name under which a work is published. A single publishing company may have multiple imprints, with the different imprints often used by the publisher to market works to different demographic consumer segments.) However, the storyline remains the same whereby the protagonists unite into a happily ever after ending.

Despite its wide appeal, these books have been criticized severely by feminists and theorists for their low literary appeal and also for confiscation and stereotyping of gender roles. According to the second wave feminists, the habit of reading romances among women tends to blind them, thus colluding within the system of oppression. Feminists have often criticized the way in which these books construct the 'image(s) of women' (Hollows 21). They argue that the image that gets created in genres of popular culture is extremely feminine that tends to infantilize women after which they are left with no sense of dignity and self-respect. In popular culture, femininity emerges with a few set of values and code of conduct which the feminists criticize for being an outcome of the patriarchal society. Such an image often becomes highly unacceptable for radical feminists who reject any practice that strengthens the difference between men and women.

On the other hand, the third generations of feminists, also called post-feminists believe that they have separate problems in comparison to the second wave feminists. They endorse femininity to some extent and also believe that the second wave feminists have imposed unfair expectations on women by proclaiming that they cannot

> wear makeup,
> shave your legs,
> wear dresses,
> have a traditional wedding or
> celebrate your femininity. (Jacob)

To the third-wave feminists, "these values are reflective of "selling out" to the patriarchal values" (*Ibid*). A popular third wave feminist Rebecca Walker mentions in her book *To Be Real: Telling the Truth and Changing the Face of Feminism*: "For many of us it seems that to be a feminist in the way that we have seen or understood feminism is to conform to an identity and way of living that doesn't allow for individuality, complexity or less than perfect personal histories." (Rebecca, qtd. Jacob)

Thus, rejecting the values of second wave feminists, she believes that since the problems vary with generations, so will their solutions and they might have to resort to practices which were unthinkable to the second wave feminists. Consequently, the complete rejection of patriarchy and the feminine values were replaced by a more liberal set of values where importance was laid on enjoyment of womanhood.

Critics of the later generations started viewing the activity of romance-reading as an important cultural practice. Janice Radway, an eminent theorist has mentioned in her work *Reading the Romance,* that all love stories are not always interpreted as romances. Mostly, romances are defined by the readers as a narrative that explores the feelings of a woman and is mostly told from her point of view. Moreover, they also enjoy the presence of explicit sexual encounters which works in the form of "verbal working out" (Hollows 79) within the narrative body. It becomes a medium for the readers to imagine themselves within the scene. Radway also conceptualizes an ideal romance as something that provided an opportunity for escape from the world that was dominated by excess of male power (*Ibid*). Besides escapism, reading also provides a room for women to proclaim their independence from all the societal responsibilities. This happens because by picking a book, a reader is able to block her surroundings and give a pleasant treat to herself. The practice of reading develops awareness among readers who feel encouraged to think about their own selves and re-evaluate their relationships. Thus, the phenomenon can be read as craving for knowledge among women rather than a simple cultural practice (ibid 82).

In this way, romance-reading developed from being a simple cultural phenomenon to a major instrument that signified the emancipation of women. Over the decades, the business generated from the Harlequin Enterprise has expanded all over the world and at present, the sales rate is over two hundred million copies a year. The information provided by Wikipedia says: "200 million Mills and Boon novels were sold globally per annum and, in the United Kingdom, one paperback was sold on average every 6.6 seconds. Mills and Boon accounted for nearly three-quarters of the British romantic fiction market in that year. Outside the UK, Mills and Boon novels were officially launched in India in 2008, although they were already popular in the country due to unofficial imports and purchases from abroad. Sales swiftly increased doubling over the 2009-2010 period."

Such a figure draws attention for a study of the socio-cultural dynamics within which these get produced. For a systematic study, three novels from the December 2012 series have been chosen for analysis. The selected year or month of publication has no special significance as the pattern continues to remain same over decades of its production. These books belong to different imprints that provide a diverse scope to the process of study. One is 'Modern'; the other is that of 'Exclusive Edition'; while the third belongs to the 'Desire' imprint. The overall plot remains same with a little difference in the way the romantic encounters get highlighted within the narrative structure. All these have rich and powerful men who lead their life in a carefree and independent manner. The only thing required in life is a soft, innocent and pure love that can melt their tough heart. This particular requirement is fulfilled by the heroine of the novels. However, the journey towards the realization of absolute love doesn't remain very easy as the characters are faced with dilemma and error in judgment because of their prior prejudices and misconception. On the other hand, the heroines are depicted as weak beings that need some powerful person to help them and come out of their problems in life which include monotony, cruelty of the society and lack of compassion. As the narrative culminates toward its end; not only the problems of their life get solved, but also those are replaced by strong, passionate and absolute love. While quoting Angela McRobbie in her book *Feminism, Femininity and Popular Culture,* Hollows argued: "feminist cultural studies' preoccupation with questions of representation should not make us ignore feminist contributions to questions about the political economy of culture, cultural policy and 'lived experience'" (McRobbie, qtd. Hollows 20). The emotional journey of the heroine and her upliftment in social status is enjoyed by women while reading the novel. The approach of the books might seem ordinary to many, but the phenomenon of reading them becomes a matter of lived experience for women. The emotional requirements of the female protagonists often match their own. Their journey from being destitute to beloved wife of some millionaire is experienced by the readers through the process of reading. Raymond Williams has argued that Cultural Studies do not always equate with "great works of art" (qtd. Hollows 68), but can often be situated within the "ordinary." Such aspects of cultural studies bring into focus many social theories and criticism which can be rightly applied to these books.

The straitjacketed manner in which the characters have been presented reinforce the conventions which have been laid down by the patriarchal society. In the beginning of *The Ruthless Caleb Wilde* one finds the hero feeling demotivated and bored in his life. Nothing was good enough to excite him, be it a glass of scotch or the women around. At this point, he got attracted towards Sage Dalton who was skimpily clad in her uniform for the evening. No other waitress seemed as attractive as her. He was particularly attracted by the grace with which she was carrying herself. In reality, Sage was uncomfortable in her dress because of its design. Nonetheless, she had to wear it as she had no other option. This virtue might have got reflected in her attitude which on the other hand got Caleb attracted towards her. Females are expected to be virtuous, warm and submissive on whom the men can take authority and control. Behaviour of a person becomes important as it creates meaning along the masculine and feminine dimensions and directs to one's gendered identity. Women who enjoy reading these novels can be assumed to be more feminine than those women who adapt aspects of masculinity. The second wave feminists have often resorted to masculine behaviours in order to remove the difference between both sexes. However, the third wave feminists consider the second wave movement to be an outcome of the patriarchal system. Mary Daly who argues against androgyny among women has pointed out that "patriarchy has even colonized feminism, producing in its place 'plastic' or 'man-made pseudo-feminism'" (qtd. Hollows 15).

The sexuality that is presented through the character of Sage Dalton can also be studied as a discourse. The discourses that these romances generate promote the 'expression' of one's sexuality. According to Michel Foucault's argument, power has a role to play in organizing and producing sexuality in a given context. Romances, on the other hand can be read as an ideological appearance that distort the notions of natural sexuality. The novel under study emphasizes the simultaneous working of both senses. The encounter starts with a simple sexual attraction towards Sage that culminates into romantic love-making as Caleb Wilde attempts to comfort her. Women who deal with the conflicts of their day-to-day life and also face repression of their sexual desire get a chance to vent out their feeling by living through the experiences of the heroine. The third person narrative structure helps the readers to place themselves in the position of the heroine. Moreover, though the readers can emotionally connect with the heroines, they feel intellectually distanced from them as they know more than them. While the heroine in most cases remain ignorant of the sexual urge that they stir among the heroes, the readers being more aware feel more confident over the entire situation. The following lines reveal the innocence of Sage, and also simultaneously increase the excitement level of the readers as they have greater knowledge over the situation: "Her knight was a determined man. . . . Caleb made her feel . . . protected. More than that. He made her feel cherished, which was a silly word to use because he was a veritable stranger" (92). Later readers find Sage in a submissive position which she enjoys as she feels protected: "The twenty-first century woman in her should have balked, but she'd loved that he had made her feel safe and wanted. He'd been her knight again" (113).

The readers of these novels are mostly modern and well-educated women who are aware about their rights and also their position in the society. However, reading these novels creates a relaxing effect that soothes them and satisfies their sexual urges. A male chauvinistic attitude is seen throughout the novel. Not only does this feeling satisfy the heroines of the novel, but also the female readers who get the opportunity to satisfy their feminine instinct in the virtual world. This attitude can be parallelled to the critiques' view of consumption culture among women. They view the departmental stores as something that operated as "female leisure centres" (Hollows 118). It provided a "feminine space in public life" (Wilson qtd. Hollows 118) where she can enjoy leisure and proclaim their liberty from the impositions that they faced in real life—either from their family and society or from the feminists who are critical about everything.

Such stereotyping of gender roles and identity has also been seen in *A Date with a Bollywood Star* where the heroine Rani has been portrayed as childish, innocent and impractical. Her readiness in taking chances with her career and a mistake that she commits toward the beginning of the story reveal the weaker side of her personality. It also justifies her parents' anxiety and desperation to help her in every situation. Perhaps even they weren't as strong a personality as the hero was. With the culmination of the story, the hero joined their life and helped them to lead a better life altogether. In one of the instances, Rani was assigned a project to interview the hero, who was a Bollywood star named Omar Khan. However, the article that she wrote was shocking even for her and revealed her unprofessional attitude to the readers. "'My God, this looks like I fancy him,' she said out loud as her eyes darted along the lines of her story" (Lakhani 28). As a serious journalist, she was not supposed to make such mistakes, but her act revealed the emotionally weaker side of her character. Despite having a strong career, the story concluded with her becoming a rich man's wife. Nothing regarding the way she must have managed her career has been mentioned in the story. Rather, it becomes evident that her rich husband must have fulfilled all her materialistic demands. This phenomenon of the heroine's settling down with a rich husband is a typical characteristic of most Mills and Boon novels. Women's profession is always considered secondary to the man's. This attitude can be attributed to the notion of the society according to which a man is considered to be bread-winner of the family. The same idea is followed in the book *Staking His Claims* by Tessa Radley. The heroine's sincerity and dedication towards her work is highlighted by her physical description.

> Despite the fact that she barely reached his shoulder when she was on her feet, she'd always seemed so formidable. Stern. Business-like. Unsmiling. Even at family occasions she dressed in a sharp, formal fashion. Dark colors—mostly black dresses with neck scarves in muted shades. (17)

This description devours her of the tender beauty that has been associated with the heroines of other Mills and Boon novels. Her marriage to the richer and more powerful Yevgeny overshadowed her profession. Moreover, the story carries reference of Yevgeny being critical of her work style to which she admitted as it was true.

> Ella shook her head again. "I'm the only one who knows all the fine details." His frustration bubbled over. "Then you have a problem—you need to learn how to delegate."
>
> "To whom? No one else . . ."
>
> "Can do the job as well as you?" He raised an eyebrow.
>
> Ella nodded slowly. "I suppose that's what I mean."
>
> "Then you have two problems—maybe more. You've surrounded yourself with the wrong people, you've failed to train

> them adequately, you don't empower your staff by giving them responsibility. Or all of the above."
>
> "None of the above." Ella's teeth snapped shut. She gave him a "take that" look. Yevgeny narrowed his gaze. "Then you're guilty of bad planning." (121)

The other book, that portrayed the heroine as an immature journalist had her act justified by the fact that she was in love. In this novel, however, a critical attitude towards the profession of the female protagonist lurked from the very beginning. This can be studied as an indirect attack on second wave feminists who have been critical about feminine behaviour as well as patriarchy. The heroine's physical description that suited her career can be connected to the physical description of second wave feminists who declined from looking beautiful. They adapted traits of masculinity which they found more humanly compared to the traits of femininity. Fashion was seen as a mode of oppression and a form of "bondage" (Hollows 139) that encouraged child labour and led women in pursuit of impossible goals towards beauty. These feminists have also been critical about women being passive consumers rather than active participants in the process of production. By posing an indirect attack on such form of feminism, these books justify the stand of feminine women who cannot give in to the impositions created by the feminists.

Many theorists are of the view that gendered behaviour is not biological; rather it is a social process. Sara Salih mentions in her work *On Judith Butler and Performativity* that "there is no 'natural body' that pre-exists its cultural inscription." (55) In the first chapter of *Gender Trouble*, Judith Butler has mentioned:

> Gender is the repeated stylization of the body, a set of repeated acts within a highly rigid regulatory frame that congeal over time to produce the appearance of substance of a natural sort of being. A political genealogy of gender ontology, if it is successful, will deconstruct the substantive appearance of gender into its constitutive acts and locate and account for those acts within the compul-

> sory frames set by various forces that police the social appearance of gender. (qtd. Salih 56)

The above argument rejects the idea of gendered behaviour as something natural. It is a result of social stereotype which gets reinforced in the novels of Mills and Boon. However, there hasn't been any strong theory that could support the above argument. On the other hand, reading of these books as leisure counts under personal choice made by women that has nothing to do with expectation made on them by the society. In sharp contrast to the above theory that argues against gendered behaviour, one has the stark figure that depicts the readership of Mills and Boon. Keeping the figure under observation, gender stereotyping and women's enjoyment of feminine pleasure cannot be outrightly rejected.

Literature plays an important role in creation of virtue within a society. An evolutionary psychologist Steven Pinker has commented in his book *The Better Angel of our Nature* that the habit of reading novels during the 18th and 19th century has reduced violence in the society—a phenomenon which he termed "humanitarian revolution" (Wells). Regarding this, he argued that the cruelty in people's heart is reduced as they get an access in the psyche and consciousness of other people. Even novelist like Jane Austen took responsibility to instigate good values within the society and infused her novels with the didactic principles. In her case, the virtues which were taught involved ethics of a bourgeoisie life that people led in middle class and upper middle class society. Though not entirely similar, the novels of Mills and Boon bear few resemblances to the novels of Austen. The similarity works in the presentation of the plot where a rich and almost spoilt hero gets tamed by love and subsequently his relationship with the heroine gets culminated into a happy ending. In most cases, the hero's change of heart takes place after realizing the innocence and purity of the heroine. On the other hand, the heroine though is mostly weak and timid, but is overladen with virtues almost every time.

In a broader sense, virtues are about good life which is achieved by a person's moral character that makes him/her do the right things at the right time and for the right reasons. Its value in literature has diminished a lot especially in the twentieth century when morality gets over-ruled by questions of political and social justice. However, in popular fiction like the novels of Mills and Boon, the readers continue to get references of the heroine's ethical code of conduct. Such is the appeal of virtue that in any given point of time, they would prefer to read about women demonstrating high sense of morality instead of degenerating values. This phenomenon can be commonly seen among readers, even if they are unable to follow those codes of conduct in their personal life. The underlying implication beyond the phenomenon is that the readers get a chance to develop a "bird's eye perspective of legislators to themselves and the world" (Wells). All the three novels which have been brought under study have plenty of instances that reveal the virtuous side of the heroines.

In *The Ruthless Caleb Wilde,* after the couple makes love, Caleb never intended to marry her or even continue the relationship. Yet, he becomes disappointed on seeing another man in her apartment. He did not even give Sage a chance to explain herself, rather left her alone after punching her friend. He felt betrayed and in order to punish her, he jumped into the occasion to settle scores with her. However, with the turn of events, they get a second chance to come closer to each other and sort out their differences.

> He nodded. Searched for words of solace . . . and instead heard himself say, "Why were you living together?"
>
> She gave a snort of disbelief.
>
> "Is that all you and your oversized ego can worry about?"

> "Answer the question," he said coldly, knowing that the ghost living inside him, the Agency operative who'd been trained to trust no one, to reject answers he expected, had suddenly taken over.
>
> "We weren't living together. Not the way you mean. David needed a place to stay with me until he found something." (107)
>
> "David and I didn't have a sexual thing going between us. We never did, never would, never could. He was gay!" (108)

This was how the outsider of the love narrative got removed and virtue was restored for the heroine. References of virtue are also found in *A Date with a Bollywood Star*, where the heroine's virtue led her into acts of innocence. Sex as an adventure is mostly discouraged among women. Protection of virginity is often equated and paralleled with protection of virtues from getting distraught. In this story, the heroine doesn't indulge herself into any kind of sexual relationship. Rather diversion of mind is brought out by her indulgence into such acts as dancing and music. "The only time she really let herself go these days was when she was dancing. She could give in to the music without having to worry about the consequences" (Lakhani 82).

Reference to her virtue could also be found in her performance of few juvenile acts that might have gone beyond the criteria of etiquettes. Also her subsequent feeling of guilt emphasizes her good character. In spite of being a 21st century woman who was taught to behave in a sophisticated manner, she found herself peeping unintentionally into Omar's bedroom for which she was overcome with the feeling of guilt. Such virtues bestowed upon women are enjoyed by female readers. It is because in an indirect manner, virtuous people are given the constructive task of building the society. In the stories, the spoilt heroes get absolutely converted into a humble and loyal person. These men also hold an important position within the society. By bringing them to their knees, the women enjoy dominance over patriarchy. Simultaneously, they also become queen of a society ruled by their lovers. With their virtues, they feel responsible to create significance within the domain.

Another attribute that has been associated with women's virtue since time immemorial is reproduction and child-rearing. One might argue that it is a form of imposition by the patriarchal society on women. This imposition not only creates a barrier for women but also on many occasions is liable to create health disorders. On this ground and many others, feminists have rejected the phenomenon of motherhood as well. Amy Richards in her article, "The Drive to Procreate: Reexamining the Biological Clock" mentions: "Some feminists have argued that the mere act of procreating is anti-woman because it perpetuates a dependence on women as biological creatures." Some also felt that the process of child-rearing confined one to their own household. Since, mostly household jobs are undermined and underrated; the tradition of women's child-rearing needed a change. Another argument that has been put forth regarding the role of women in child-birth and child-rearing is related to the concept of poverty. Women already earn lesser than men in any given sector. Child-birth and health issues create a tendency towards unemployment. Even after the phase is crossed, child-rearing is a phenomenon that creates unemployment and poverty among women. The tendency to give the best to their children is always present among parents and especially among women. This attitude creates a further possibility of deterioration in their lifestyle. However, in spite of all that, women themselves want to reproduce and procreate on the basis of their personal choice even while being oblivious to the society's expectation from them.

The problems discussed above while dealing with the feminist argument have mostly been depicted in the novels which have been brought together for study. In *The Ruthless Caleb Wilde*, Sage becomes pregnant after having an intercourse with Caleb Wilde. Later on, she faces difficulty for being a single parent which also included her difficulty for being poorly employed. To add to her injuries, she faced challenge from a rich man who claimed the baby to be his grandchild. However, all the problems get sorted out when Caleb re-entered her life and gave her all sorts of protection and comfort. Not only, did he solve her problems, but also helped her out of her poverty by making her his wife. As a wife to Caleb Wilde, poverty was replaced by richness which she could enjoy all her life. In the novel *Staking His Claims,* the problems of child-birth and child-rearing have been complicated by bringing in the concept of surrogacy. The attitude of seeking the best for one's child is seen in the story as the heroine Ella was looking for a foster home for her baby. She wanted her surrogate child to receive the best family for adoption. This attitude in her led to rejection of Yevgeny Volkovoy as a prospective father to her child which became a ground of struggle for both of them and subsequently led to the development of the plot. Ella's reluctance in keeping the baby with herself and her more concentration in her work through the child was justified by the fact that she had been through a traumatic experience in her childhood that changed her outlook towards life and converted her into a rough person.

To conclude, it would be right to say that Mills and Boon, though reinforces patriarchy at the superficial level but is actually remarkable for bringing out texts which are fundamental for the understanding of post-feminism. In her book *Feminism, Femininity and Popular Culture,* Joanne Hollows goes to the extent of calling these stories revenge narratives. She comments: "the way in which the Harlequin heroine brings the contemptuous hero to his knees not only challenges the common assumption that the romantic heroine is passive and childlike, but it also "conceals a deep-seated desire for vengeance." In this way, romantic fiction does not simply portray feminine passivity, but also contains powerful 'revenge fantasies' and therefore is a form of protest, even though this anger is eventually neutralized." (76)

# Works Cited

Adrianes, Fien. "Post Feminism in Popular Culture: A Potential for Critical Resistance." *Politics and Culture* 4 (Nov. 2009). Politicsandculture.org/2009/11/09/post-feminism-in-popular-culture-a-potential-for-critical-resistance/>

_____. "Feminist Perspectives on Reproduction and the Family." *Stanford Encyclopedia of Philosophy*. 6 Nov. 2004. <http: //plato. stanford.edu/ entries/feminism-family/>

Fox-Genovese, Elizabeth. *Feminism without Illusions: A Critique of Individualism*. USA: University of North Carolina Press, 1991.

Hollows, Joanne. *Feminism, Femininity and Popular Culture*. Manchester and New York: Manchester University Press, 2000.

Lakhani, Riya. *Date with a Bollywood Star*. Mumbai: Harlequin, 2012.

Marton, Sandra. *The Ruthless Caleb Wilde*. Mumbai: Harlequin, 2012.

Pearce, Lynne. "Popular Romance and its Readers." *A Companion to Romance: From Classical to Contemporary*, ed. Corinne Saunders. 521-38. USA: Blackwell, 2004.

Radley, Tessa. *Staking His Claims*. Mumbai: Harlequin, 2012.

Ramsdell, Kristin. *Romance Fiction: A Guide to the Genre*. USA: Genreflecting Advisory Series, 2012.

Wells, Thomas. "Reading Jane Austen as a Moral Philosopher." *The Philosopher's Beard: Essays in Philosophy, Politics and Economics*. Feb. 2012. <http: //www.philosophersbeard.org/2011/08/jane-austen-terrible-novelist-brilliant.html>

Richards, Amy. "The Drive to Procreate: Re-examining the Biological Clock." *General Women & Feminism*. 2008. <http: //plato. stanford.edu/entries/feminism-family/>

Salih, Sara. "On Judith Butler and Performativity." *Judith Butler*. 7 Aug. 2006: 55-68. <faculty.georgetown.edu/. . ./Salih-Butler-Performativity-Chapter_3.pdf>

Stets, Jan E., and Peter J. Burke. "Femininity/Masculinity." *Encyclopedia of Sociology*. Revised Ed. Eds. Edgar F. Borgatta and Rhonda J.V. Montgomery. 997-1005. New York: Macmillan.

"Mills & Boon." *Wikipedia, The Free Encyclopedia*.

"Imprint (trade name)." *Wikipedia, The Free Encyclopedia*.

# Feminist Gothic in Charlotte Perkins Gilman's "The Yellow Wallpaper"

**MEGHANA J.R.**
**Res. and Teaching Asst., Kuvempu University, Shivamogga**

Charlotte Pekins Gilman wrote the short story "The Yellow Wallpaper" in 1892. She had no way of knowing that the story would one day be regarded as a classic in feminist literature. The Gothic tale of "The Yellow Wallpaper" had become just that, although it took nearly a century to find a truly understanding audience. Early readers were appreciative of the tale and indeed it still stands as a wonderful example of the genre. Although the autobiographical aspects of "The Yellow Wallpaper" are compelling it is the symbolism and underlying feminist connotations that led best to discussion first is John, the narrator's husband. He could be viewed as the patriarchy itself, as Beverly Hume says with his dismissal of all but the tangible and constant condescension to his wife. It is true that husband's language is exaggerated at times but dismissing the husband's character as caricature seems extreme. Woman feels trapped, her unwanted nursery room is ugly and the windows are barred; this was once a precaution for children inhabiting the nursery, but now makes a cage like environment for the narrator and serves as a constant reminder of children.

In this paper we are going to discuss about the Gothic elements in this short story. "The Yellow Wallpaper" is a semi-autobiographical short story in which Gilman describes the treatment of women during a rest cure prescribed for nervous disorders by Dr. Silas Weir Mitchell, who was a famous physician. The story describes the submissive, childlike obedience of women to male authority figures that was considered typical at the beginning of the twentieth century.

The story, written just after the Romantic period, is full of gothic element and images. Blindly blamed on mental illness or a medical condition, the slow deterioration of the protagonist can be traced back to discontentment and entrapment within marriage. She is plagued by the societal designation of who she should be and her role in the marriage and household. The home and marriage are all linked with gothic images that foreshadow the outcome of the main character's problematic marriage.

The unnamed protagonist of the story is helpless to express her own needs. She is taken by her husband, John, to a country house so that she can recuperate from a nervous condition. The reader is immediately aware of the condescending attitude of the physician husband toward his wife. She is relegated against her will to a third floor room of the house, a room that the owners previously used as a nursery. Symbolically, the room with the yellow wallpaper serves as a prison where the wife is restricted, like a child, from the intellectual activities of reading and writing. At first, the narrator rebels against the constraints by keeping a secret diary. When John discovers her disobedience, she is chastised and her diary is cruelly destroyed.

Social interactions are also held to a minimum. Since the husband lectures in other cities, the narrator is often left without emotional support for days at a time. When John is at home, his conversations are patronizing, and he dismisses her concerns about her condition. Clearly, her role is to comfort him and trust blindly that her own condition is improving. John's self-absorption does not permit him to see that his wife's condition is deteriorating. Jennie (John's sister), who manages the household, is another example of the restricted role of women. She busies herself with decorating and supervising the kitchen. She unquestioningly carries out John's orders to monitor the narrator's activities, even when her own contacts with the woman make it clear that what the doctor orders is not what the patient needs. She nevertheless obeys blindly until it is too late to reverse the effects of the narrator's descent into madness.

The colour of the wallpaper in the room where the protagonist of the story stayed also carries with it some gothic elements. "While the gothic is usually described in terms of light and dark, there is something menacing about the wallpaper's yellow colour, representing something stale, old and decayed." The yellow is described as "a smouldering unclean yellow" that is "strangely faded by slow-turning sunlight." Her use of the word, "smouldering," meaning being in a state of suppressed activity, suggests she thought the same of her marriage to John. There is also something dark and gothic in nature about the suppression and "unclean" colour. From the beginning of the story, the colonial mansion is described as a "haunted house," leaning toward gothic evidences. In addition to the colour of the wallpaper, the room in which she's kept seems to evoke feelings that it's a haunted space, even if it's only haunted by the protagonist herself.

The wallpaper seems to spawn more haunting and gothic images when the protagonist says, "There are things in that paper that nobody knows about or ever will." She claims, "Behind that outside pattern the dim shapes get clearer every day." Later, she notices a "woman stooping down and creeping about behind that pattern." She says she sees bars within the wallpaper when she mentions, "at night in any kind of light, in twilight, candlelight, lamplight, and worst of all by moonlight, it becomes bars! The outside pattern I mean, and the woman behind it is as plain as can be." Whether representative of her declining mental faculties or her desperation to leave her marriage and the societal standards of the time behind, there is something evocative about the images she sees within the wallpaper.

The protagonist is nameless and thus, powerless to her predicament. Her repressed desire to leave her marriage makes this item, otherwise not of particular interest, noteworthy. The overarching idea of being trapped in her marriage and in the "great immovable bed" that she's kept in represents non-traditional gothic images. If the mental faculties are in question, both the nameless protagonist and the woman in the wallpaper are split personalities. Later, the one woman becomes many when the protagonist says, "there are so many of those creeping women and they creep so fast," suggesting many personalities or factions of her identity. When she tears the paper off the wall and frees this manifestation of a woman, she believes that she frees herself. This haunting disconnect in her mental health and her continuous connection with the woman in the wallpaper suggests the protagonist represents a gothic character. While images in "The Yellow Wallpaper" don't necessarily fit the conventional definition of the gothic, they definitely lean toward something unknown and haunted. The manner in which the protagonist's husband, John, keeps her in a room to "rest" is haunting enough but the additional elements within the room and the wallpaper lead to an unsettling feeling.

The powerful pattern in the yellow wallpaper resembles bars that confine the protagonist in her world of loneliness, helplessness, and infantilism. Deprived of intellectual stimulation, the narrator's imagination conjures up a world behind the paper where captive women wait helplessly to be freed. Ironically, she is one of the women seeking to be liberated. Destroying the paper seems to be the only way she can destroy the hold of stifling mores that demand female subservience to men and free women from male dominance. Charlotte Perkins Gilman had no way of knowing that a story she wrote in 1892 would one day be regarded as a classic in feminist literature. The gothic tale of "The Yellow Wallpaper" has become just that, although it took nearly a century to find a truly understanding audience. Early readers were appreciative of the sheer horror of the tale, and, indeed, it still stands as a wonderful example of the genre. But it was not until the rediscovery of the story in the early 1970s that "The Yellow Wallpaper" was recognized as an early feminist indictment of Victorian patriarchy. This story contains many typical gothic trappings, but beneath the conventional façade lies a tale of repression and freedom told in intricate symbolism as seen through the eyes of a mad narrator.

It is difficult to discuss the meaning in this story without first examining the author's own personal experience. "The Yellow Wallpaper" gives an account of a woman driven to madness as a result of the Victorian "rest-cure," a once frequently prescribed period of inactivity thought to cure hysteria and nervous conditions in women. As Gary Scharnhorst points out, this treatment originated with Dr. Weir Mitchell, who personally prescribed this "cure" to Gilman herself. She was in fact driven to near madness and later claimed to have written "The Yellow Wallpaper" to protest this treatment of women like herself, and specifically to address Dr. Weir Mitchell with a "propaganda piece." A copy of the story was actually sent to Mitchell, and although he never replied to Gilman personally, he is said to have confessed to a friend that he had changed his treatment of hysterics after reading the story.

Although the autobiographical aspects of "The Yellow Wallpaper" are compelling, it is the symbolism and the underlying feminist connotations that lead best to discussion. First is John, the narrator's husband. He could be viewed as the patriarchy itself, as Beverly Hume says, with his dismissal of all but the tangible and his constant condescension to his wife, but some critics have viewed this character as near-caricature. Many of the passages concerning the husband can be interpreted as containing sarcasm, a great many contain irony, and several border on parody. It is true that the husband's language is exaggerated at times, but dismissing the husband's character as caricature seems extreme. He is instead the natural complement to the narrator's madness and uncontrolled fancy: the character of John is control and "sanity" as defined by Victorian culture and is therefore the narrator's opposite. Greg Johnson notes that John exhibits a near-obsession with "reason," even as his wife grows mad. He is the narrator's necessary counterpart, without whose stifling influence, her eventual freedom would not be gained. And he is also transformed at the end of the tale—in a reversal of traditional gothic roles—because it is he, not a female, who faints when confronted with madness.

Central to the story is the wallpaper itself. It is within the wallpaper that the narrator finds her hidden self and her eventual damnation/ freedom. Her obsession with the paper begins subtly and then consumes both the narrator and the story. Once settled in the long-empty "ancestral estate," a typical gothic setting, the narrator is dismayed to learn that her husband has chosen the top-floor nursery room for her. The room is papered in horrible yellow wallpaper, the design of which "commit[s] every artistic sin." The design begins to fascinate the narrator and she begins to see more than just the outer design. At first she sees "bulbous eyes" and "absurd unblinking eyes . . . everywhere," phrases suggestive to John Bak of a panopticon, an "alternative" prison developed by Jeremy Bentham in the nineteenth century to replace the dank English prison of the time (39). Further, according to Bak, this new prison, as described by Michael Foucault in *Discipline and Punish* (1975), involved observance of prisoners at all times (40). This all-seeing prison symbolism is echoed according to Bak in the narrator's observation of "gates that lock" and the constant surveillance of John and the housekeeper, Jennie (42). Bak goes on to suggest that the nursery room, with its barred windows and rings in the wall, was designed for the restraint of mental patients, but other critics assert that these were in fact common safety precautions used in Victorian nurseries and that such interpretations are extreme.

The wallpaper gradually consumes the narrator's being, offering up more complex images as time passes. She first notices a different coloured sub-pattern of a figure beneath the "front design." This figure is eventually seen as a woman who "creeps" and shakes the outer pattern, now seen by the narrator as bars. Gary Scharnhorst says that this woman-figure becomes essentially the narrator's "doppelganger," or double, trapped behind the bars of her role in the patriarchy (17). As the story progresses, the narrator identifies more and more with the figure in the wallpaper, until she refers to herself in the third person. In this statement the narrator says, "I've got out at last, said I, in spite of you and Jane"; this statement allows for many different interpretations—some of which change the entire nature of the story, or at least the very ending. Probably the most common interpretation of this line assumes Jane to be the previously unmentioned name of the narrator. This seems by far the simplest and most reasonable explanation, but this brief statement has produced some wild theories ranging in scope from a misprint of the name "Jennie" or "Julia" to a deliberate connection to *Jane Eyre* by Charlotte Bronte (Owens 76-77). There are indeed parallels between the madwoman in *Jane Eyre* and the madness exhibited by the narrator in "The Yellow Wallpaper," but it seems unlikely that the more unusual theories would bear up under close scrutiny. With that in mind, we will assume for convenience sake that the name Jane does in fact refer to the narrator herself.

Another feature of the prison/ nursery in which the narrator observes her wallpaper is the heavy bedstead, which is nailed to the floor. The interpretations of this feature are variations on a theme, ranging from an image of the narrator's "static sexuality" (Scharnhorst 19) to "a sexual crucifixion" (Johnson 526). These statements ring true regarding Victorian sexuality; it was as immobile as the unmoving bedstead. A Victorian wife belonged to her husband and her body was his to do with whatever he pleased. Victorian women were counselled that conjugal relations were a woman's duty simply to be borne until a sufficient number of children arrived and it was no longer necessary. In this context, the image of the nailed-down bed becomes perhaps the most understandable symbol in the entire story.

What of the narrator herself and her madness? An interesting way to view her actions is, in the words of Greg Johnson, "an expression of long-suppressed rage." Johnson goes on to suggest that the narrator's madness may in fact be temporary, as the author's own breakdown was in real life. The narrator is presented as an artist and a writer and it is through her writing, Johnson says, that her suppressed rage becomes apparent. There is further justification in believing her madness to be temporary. After the narrator becomes free/ becomes the creeping woman in the paper, she says, "I suppose I shall have to get back behind the pattern when it comes night, and that is hard!" Since the narrator had seen the pattern as bars with the creeping figure behind them, perhaps this statement may allude to an eventual return to a societal norm of behavior: Jane, the narrator, may get back behind the bars of Victorian womanhood, but "that is hard!"

There is also the interesting connection between the mad narrator of "The Yellow Wallpaper" and the character of Bertha Mason, the madwoman in the attic in Charlotte Bronte's *Jane Eyre*. Almost all writings on the story have alluded to this connection; some discuss it at length. Perhaps the comparison is inevitable, as Bertha Mason is probably the most well-known example of a gothic madwoman. When viewed as a polarized or split identity, the link between Jane Eyre/ Bertha Mason and Narrator Jane/ Wallpaper figure is quite clear. The first in both pairs is the conventional self, the "rational self," and the second is "the raging and uncontrolled madwoman" (Owens 77). Greg Johnson says it is the anger, the boiling rage, of these alter egos that results in eventual triumph over their patriarchal influences. By reading "The Yellow Wallpaper" in this light, we can view the story as an interaction between the protagonist and her "shadow self" (King and Morris 29). There is another similarity between Bertha Mason and the narrator of our tale: they both "creep," or crawl about on all fours. This may be identification with animal behaviour or a way to explain that both characters have lost touch with civilization or patriarchy. However, as King and Morris add, it may simply be an expression of the narrator's "self-suppression," a suppression carried to the point of regression: the narrator ends the story sleeping most of the day and creeping around a nursery room like an infant (30).

Bronte's madwoman may be more animal than infant, but the opposite is more likely true of our narrator. The question of the narrator's fate still remains. Is she truly an unreliable narrator, sinking steadily into irretrievable madness? Or is she exhibiting the only sane response to an insane world order? Does she find doom in her madness? Or triumph and freedom at last? The story cannot be viewed in purely supernatural terms, with a real phantom behind the wallpaper; thus the narrator's madness is undeniable. However, as both Johnson and King and Morris point out, it is this response which grants her freedom in the end. It is her rebellion which is her redemption, and even if her conventional self is completely obliterated, her "survival" is assured by the survival of her writing, her text. As we read the story, the narrator "reads" the wallpaper, and she sees in it her own "suppressed self" (King and Morris 32). So when the narrator destroys the paper and pulls it down in the end, it might be symbolic of the destruction of her other self.

In fact, it is significant that the entire story revolves around wallpaper, which would be considered by many to be merely feminine frivolity. Greg Johnson recounts a story in "Gilman's Gothic Allegory: Rage and Redemption in 'The Yellow Wallpaper'" about Emily Dickinson's mother. In the story, the pregnant woman had requested that the wallpaper be changed in her room. When denied the change by her husband, the woman secretly arranged the re-papering herself, her "only recorded act of wifely defiance." The Victorian wife had so little control over her own life that it was through these "frivolities" such as clothing and even wallpaper that these women exercised their autonomy. It seems significant, therefore, that the narrator's madness is expressed through the chiefly feminine symbol of wallpaper. "The Yellow Wallpaper," though a wonderful and frightening gothic tale, will probably continue to be thought of in feminist terms. Modern women, by reading such texts, can gain a new perspective on our present situation. We can also learn to avoid past pitfalls. By understanding the madness in "The Yellow Wallpaper," we can perhaps prevent such psychic horrors in the future.

In examining Gilman's "The Yellow Wallpaper" as a work of Female Gothic, the following essay acts, to some degree, as a corrective to Johnson's essay and to the numerous studies that have read this story exclusively as a light and non-political horror tale or as a politically charged feminist piece that explores the ideology of femininity. Their common oversight has been to fail to consider the suitability and implications of Gilman's choice of what later came to be classified as the Female Gothic mode, a form that is generally distinguished from the traditional Gothic mode as it centres its lens on a young woman's rite of passage into womanhood and her ambivalent relationship to contemporary domestic ideology, especially the joint institutions of marriage and motherhood. As such, the Female Gothic deploys the supernatural for political ends. "The Yellow Wallpaper" not only haunts the predominantly male Gothic tradition in America but is, itself, haunted by that tradition. There are various literary ghosts deriving from the works of such authors as Brockden Brown, Poe, and Hawthorne, which I hope to identify and expose, haunting the ancestral halls that John and his wife rent for the summer. This hereditary estate may be read meta-fictionally as the Gothic tradition. Just as her narrator earnestly strips away wallpaper in an attempt to improve the "atrocious nursery," Gilman is engaged in renovating an extremely popular and well-established house of fiction. Indeed, according to Leslie Fiedler in his seminal study, *Love and Death in the American Novel* (1960), which, among other things, theorizes about the implications of Gothic literature's transplantation from British to American soil, the Gothic nature of American literature has always been pre-eminent. In his words, "of all the fiction of the West, our own [American fiction] is most deeply influenced by the gothic, is almost essentially a gothic one" (129). As the relationship between gender and genre is vital and frequently under analyzed in the examination of American Gothic—and Fiedler is equally guilty on this count as he conceives of Gothic literature in the American tradition as a male form that merely protests against women and is marked by a flight from the domestic and the feminine—the question of gender will be brought to bear on both Fiedler's comments and Gilman's incursions into what is largely, in American literature, prior to the publication of "The Yellow Wallpaper," an established male tradition. Although, as Alison Milbank has noted, "Gothic writing has been conceived of in gendered terms" since its inception in the eighteenth century, theorizing about the gendered aspects of this genre is a more recent phenomenon that began after Ellen Moers coined the term "Female Gothic" in her classic 1976 study, *Literary Women*, in reference to a mode of literature that taps women's fears about sexuality and childbirth. Such gender-aware theorizing was also undertaken, almost concurrently, within other genres. Just as theorists of the female bildungsroman (novel of development) illustrated how gender is a vital component in that genre as the ideal of success is gender-contingent, and men and women tend to be impeded and judged in different ways by their societies, theorists of the female Gothic called attention to the fact that women's generally repressed fears and desires—Gothic's twin fascinations—differ quite dramatically from those of their male counterparts.

Charlotte Perkins Gilman's "The Yellow Wallpaper" has been interpreted in many ways over the years. Modernist critics have applied depth psychology to the story and written about the symbolism of sexual repression in the nursery bars, the chained-down bed, and the wallpaper. Genre critics have discussed the story as an example of supernatural gothic fiction, in which a ghost actually haunts the narrator. But most importantly, feminist critics (re)discovered the story in the 1970s and interpreted it as a critique of a society that subjugated women into the role of wife and mother and repressed them so much that all they could ever hope to be was an "angel in the house."

It is significant however, that the narrator herself had absolutely no say in this matter. She was never asked if she thought that it would be of help to spend time in the country. She was never consulted about whether or not it could be her writing that is causing her emotional difficulties. Instead, the men who have power over her decided these things for her, locking her in a nursery and forbidding her to write. Whereas before she was figuratively locked into the role of wife and mother, she is now physically locked into the uppermost room of the summerhouse. Just as she has never been able to leave her prescribed social role, now she cannot leave her wallpapered prison. The narrator's imprisonment echoes all the way back to the female Gothic's classic beginnings in Anne Radcliffe's *The Mysteries of Udolpho*. Instead of being locked away "in a foreign land ... surrounded by vice and violence," the narrator is locked away by the man who should be closest to her and is surrounded by the oppressive patriarchal power structure of her time (Delamotte 206).

The narrator of "The Yellow Wallpaper" is a paradox; as she loses touch with the outer world, she comes to a greater understanding of the inner reality of her life. This inner/outer split is crucial to understanding the nature of the narrator's suffering. At every point, she is faced with relationships, objects, and situations that seem innocent and natural but that are actually quite bizarre and even oppressive. In a sense, the plot of "The Yellow Wallpaper" is the narrator's attempt to *avoid* acknowledging the extent to which her external situation stifles her inner impulses. From the beginning, we see that the narrator is an imaginative, highly expressive woman. She remembers terrifying herself with imaginary night-time monsters as a child, and she enjoys the notion that the house they have taken is haunted. Yet as part of her "cure," her husband forbids her to exercise her imagination in any way. Both her reason and her emotions rebel at this treatment, and she turns her imagination onto seemingly neutral objects—the house and the wallpaper—in an attempt to ignore her growing frustration. Her negative feelings colour her description of her surroundings, making them seem uncanny and sinister, and she becomes fixated on the wallpaper.

As the narrator sinks further into her inner fascination with the wallpaper, she becomes progressively more dissociated from her day-to-day life. This process of dissociation begins when the story does, at the very moment she decides to keep a secret diary as "a relief to her mind." From that point, her true thoughts are hidden from the outer world, and the narrator begins to slip into a fantasy world in which the nature of "her situation" is made clear in symbolic terms. Gilman shows us this division in the narrator's consciousness by having the narrator puzzle over effects in the world that she herself has caused. For example, the narrator doesn't immediately understand that the yellow stains on her clothing and the long "smooch" on the wallpaper are connected. Similarly, the narrator fights the realization that the predicament of the woman in the wallpaper is a symbolic version of her own situation. At first she even disapproves of the woman's efforts to escape and intends to "tie her up."

When the narrator finally identifies herself with the woman trapped in the wallpaper, she is able to see that other women are forced to creep and hide behind the domestic "patterns" of their lives, and that she herself is the one in need of rescue. The horror of this story is that the narrator must lose herself to understand herself. She has untangled the pattern of her life, but she has torn herself apart in getting free of it. An odd detail at the end of the story reveals how much the narrator has sacrificed. During her final split from reality, the narrator says, "I've got out at last, in spite of you and Jane." Who is this Jane? Some critics claim "Jane" is a misprint for "Jennie," the sister-in-law. It is more likely, however, that "Jane" is the name of the unnamed narrator, who has been a stranger to herself and her jailers. Now she is horribly "free" of the constraints of her marriage, her society, and her own efforts to repress her mind.

Finally the narrator gives way to madness, ripping at the wallpaper and creeping around the room, causing her husband to faint. She hasn't managed to escape the confines of her relationship yet she is attempting to free the woman from behind the pattern of the wallpaper is directly co-related to her desire for control within her life and relationships, she can assert her dominance over the wallpaper yet she is incapable of changing her relationship. It highlights the patriarchal male domination and also gothic elements and submissive women in the short story. As a famous writer said: "A woman should go against the patriarchal society otherwise she should go mad."

# Obesity as Grotesque: The Inscribed Female Body in Margaret Atwood's *Lady Oracle*

**SANGEETHA PUTHIYEDATH**
**The English and Foreign Languages University, Hyderabad**

Joan Foster, the foster child of destiny, a trapeze artist who swings from identity to identity, assumes multiple roles in the course of her life, but is mistress of none. Joan, the narrator of *Lady Oracle*, is the daughter of an ambitious social climbing mother. Joan's childhood is blighted by her mother's ruthless desire to mould her into an object to hold up to society's appreciation. Joan successfully thwarts her by indulging in an eating spree gaining hundreds of pounds. Joan uses eating as a weapon. "I swelled visibly, relentlessly, before her very eyes, I rose like dough, my body advanced inch by inch towards her across the dining-room table, in this at least I was undefeated" (70). "The war between myself and my mother was on in earnest; the disputed territory was my body" (69). Though successful in her struggle with her mother, Joan perceives quite early in her childhood that society had rigid rules about female beauty and that anyone who challenges those precepts are blanked out by society. Rejecting the ideal shape she eats herself out of society's idea of girlhood.

Joan's realization that the more she grows the less visibility she has, is cemented by her experience in the dance class. Though Joan longs to dance as a butterfly with beautiful cellophane wings in "The Butterfly Frolic," her favourite dance in the school recital, she is condemned to stomp around in a teddy-bear suit in a specially created role of the mothball. Throwing herself whole-heartedly into her new role, and dancing in a frenzy, "It was a dance of rage and destruction, tears rolled down my cheeks behind the fur, the butterflies would die," (50) she is nevertheless bitterly disappointed. "As she expresses her rage against the slender, graceful butterflies, she acts out her rebellion against the rules of femininity that dictate acceptable body shape and movements," observes Bouson (67). But she also feels "naked and exposed, as if this ridiculous dance was the truth about me and everyone could see it" (50). The image of a butterfly hidden and trapped in the bulk of a mothball waiting to break free is a fitting symbol for Joan who later sees herself in the mirror "the outline of [her] former body" surrounding her "like a mist, like a phantom moon, like the image of Dumbo the Flying Elephant superimposed on [her] own" (214). Joan realizes that conversions are hardly easy and discarded skins have a habit of reclaiming bodies when one least expects it.

Joan's rejection from the circle of dancers is later re-enacted in the persecution she suffers as a Brownie. Psychologically, it leaves a deeper scar than her experience with the butterfly dance. Joan is forced to become a Brownie by her mother who hopes that the company of other children will make her daughter more sociable and might prod her into shedding some weight. Atwood uses this to explore the devious ways by which children, especially girls torment weaker girls. Elizabeth, Marlene and Lynne, her fellow Brownies, with unconscious cruelty systematically torture Joan. Atwood suggests that bullying among girls is more corrosive than bullying among boys because it was so relentless and insidious. Joan's so-called friends exploit her need for friendship and her fear of the ravine by ordering her to do their bidding. They often ran off leaving her frightened and alone but claimed "that their running off was a punishment, deserved by me, for something I had done or hadn't done that day: I had skipped too heavily in the fairy ring, I hadn't stood straight enough, my tie was rumpled, I had dirty fingernails, I was fat" (59). Joan's friends like her mother and the rest of the society were punishing her for not conforming to the norm of ideal girlhood.

Joan's fat body, unhealthily bloated, padded with layers of fat, can be seen as a desperate attempt to insulate herself from the psychological scars her mother inflicts on her. Obviously an unplanned and unwanted child, Joan is a source of constant disappointment to her mother. Realizing that the only manner in which she can touch her mother is not through love but through embarrassment, Joan maximizes the humiliation she can heap on her by being fat and clumsy and perceives her bulk as a "refutation" of her mother and a "victory" over her. "It was only in relation to my mother that I derived a morose pleasure from my weight," observes Joan perceptively "in relation to everyone else, including my father, it made me miserable" (74). Using her body to punish her mother proves to be a double-edged sword, one that draws blood, not only from her mother but also from herself. It makes her life very lonely and excludes her from normal childhood activities. It also makes her a butt of mean pranks by other children.

Joan's massive bulk blights her adolescence as well. By the time she was fifteen she "was five feet eight . . . and . . . weighed two hundred and forty-five . . . pounds" (74). Joan's size banishes her from the circle of normalcy and renders her invisible to the members of the opposite sex. Her female classmates seek her company while meeting boys because her bulk shows them off to their advantage and she is not perceived as a threat to them. They along with the young men de-sex her and her so-called "sexual experiences" in adolescence are ludicrous—a boy seeking comfort by burying his face in her stomach after he was rejected by the girl he was pursuing and a proposal for marriage by a much older man. Joan buys acceptance from her peers by suppressing all her emotions and playing the role of an 'agony aunt,' one in whom they can confide their worries and discuss their fears. An emotionally starved Joan seeks vicarious enjoyment by watching tragic romantic dramas on the screen in the company of her Aunt Lou. Banished from normal activities because of her bulk Joan desperately seeks a role that she can fulfil as an adult.

Joan's obesity serves as a "magic cloak of blubber and invisibility" (141) that allow her to elude the voyeuristic male gaze cancelling the social control of men in the process. The invisibility that it confers on her ultimately proves to be empowering. Joan experiences men, not "as aggressive lechers but as bashful, elusive creatures who could think of nothing to say to me and who faded away at my approach" (140). In a comic inversion an adolescent Joan realizes that unlike her Brownie days she no longer has to fear anything from male molesters lurking near the ravines and she "would be able to squash any potential molester against a wall merely by breathing out" (140). Her bulk empowers her and when the European cook at Bite-a-Bit proposes to her she imagines herself bearing down the aisle in white satin, "with this tiny foreign man slung over my arm like a purse" (100). This incongruous image is extended to ludicrous lengths when she daydreams about having sex with him, and she envisions him as "scurrying" over her body like a friendly furry animal, her body as "enormous to him as a peninsula" (102).

Though *Lady Oracle* through a carnivalesque inversion empowers the obese female body thus resisting the controlling power that masculinity exerts over the female form, it also raises unsettling questions. The "Fat Lady" is on display at the Exhibition not as an object of admiration, but because her 'fatness' is considered unnatural. In a recurring fantasy, Joan imagines the Fat Lady in a ballerina costume proceeding inch by inch across Canada on a high wire (103). In a variation of this fantasy, Joan envisions a fat woman on a stage in a harem costume doing a striptease: "She'd start taking off her clothes, while I watched, powerless to stop her. She'd wobble her hips, removing her veils, one after another, but no one would whistle, no one would yell *Take it off baby*. I tried to turn off these out-of-control fantasies, but couldn't, I had to watch them through to the end" (251).

Joan's anxiety about her fatness and her embarrassment with her body finds expression in these uncontrolled recurring fantasies. It is hardly surprising that an embattled Joan at Terremoto, lonely and threatened is traumatized once again by the Fat Lady fantasies though she is no longer fat. She imagines that Mr. Vitroni her landlord will keep her in a cage, fatten her up, dress her in black satin underwear, and then charge admission to the village men who want to see her. Imagining herself turning into "one of those Fellini whores, gigantic and shapeless," she envisions herself spending the rest of her life "in a cage, as a fat whore, a captive Earth Mother for whom somebody else collected the admission tickets" (328). Imagining herself turning into "one of those Fellini whores, gigantic and shapeless," she envisions herself spending the rest of her life "in a cage, as a fat whore, a captive Earth Mother for whom somebody else collected the admission tickets" (328).

Unlike Joan and her mother, Aunt Lou, is presented as someone who is comfortable with her body and bodily functions. Significantly, she works for an organisation that helps dispel doubts about the functions of the female body. Positioned in opposition to her mother in the narrative Aunt Lou is the only person Joan can relate to; who, to an extent, fulfils her need for a maternal figure. Abandoned by a gambling husband in her youth, Aunt Lou educated herself and found a job. Unlike her mother who obsesses about what others think and spends her time trying to impress others, her aunt is nonchalant about the views of others and live and dress in a manner that she finds comfortable.

She disregards the rules of the society and for this reason is banished from the house parties Joan's mother periodically holds. Joan finds in her a kindred spirit and adopts her as a role model.

More importantly Aunt Lou also provides Joan a means of escape. With remarkable insight Lou stipulates that Joan will inherit her legacy only if she loses weight. Given the incentive of freedom, a determined Joan drastically reduces her weight and escapes her mother's clutches to fly to England. Along with the fat that she sheds, she sloughs off her identity and assumes a new name and identity and even acquires a passport in her new name. Her substitution of one identity with another which she had always indulged in now assumes a more serious and menacing dimension—one that can result in prosecution and incarceration if detected. The irony is definitely at her expense when she admits blandly much later when as a married woman she embarks on an affair with Chuck Brewer, "this was the beginning of my double life" (246).

"Joan is nothing if not a self-caricaturist as well as a product of Gothic romance conventions, as she switches between real life and fantasy roles in a continual process of double coding" remarks Howells (66). Joan's encounter with the Polish Count is symptomatic of her dealings with other people, especially her romantic liaisons. She suppresses aspects of herself and her past from people and only reveals what she decides that a particular person will approve. Joan's deeply ingrained unhappiness with herself, based on what she considers as societal approval, impels her to presume that other people will be equally condemnatory of her past as well as her character. This fear of disapproval and a compulsion to win acceptance forces her to block certain aspects while simultaneously highlighting other aspects of her character. This game of shifting identities which she successfully carried on as a teenager at high school becomes impossible to sustain in an adult world where relationships are by necessity more complex. The fear of censure by a patriarchal society blights Joan's relationships and even her marriage.

"Only when Joan stops filling her mouth with food does she begin writing, and this raises further questions concerning the links Atwood forges between "body" and "text," observes Davies in her article "Margaret Atwood's female bodies" (Howells 65). The link between suppressed emotions, the silenced words and the unexpressed rebellion and Joan's weight is hard to overlook. It almost appears as though her interiority filled to bursting by her unvoiced unhappiness and pain has exteriorised itself as the layers of fat that pad her body.

A woman's body is presented by Margaret Atwood as heavily inscribed by the culture in which she finds herself in. Compelled to constantly measure and judge herself against the proscription that deny acceptance to a woman's body, if it does not conform to male determined precepts of beauty, the body becomes an important intermediary in a woman's dialogue with society and a tool with which she negotiates her relationship with the outside society. The pressure to present oneself as an object of desire for the male gaze—(Here one cannot but assert the ubiquitous nature of the male gaze because even the women have internalized the male gaze)—puts enormous pressure on women. This pressure expresses itself as eating disorders *anorexia* and *bulimia nervosa*. While Atwood unpacks the frightening escalation of *anorexia* in *Edible Woman*, she explores another facet of eating disorder in *Lady Oracle*. In both these texts she explores how women who feel trapped by a patriarchal order use their body as an instrument to record their protest.

## Bibliography

Atwood, Margaret. *Lady Oracle*. London: Andre Deutsch, 1977.

Butler, Judith. *Gender Trouble: Feminism and the Subversion of Identity*. New York: Routledge, 2010.

Bouson, Brooks J. *Brutal Choreographies: Oppositional Strategies and Narrative Design in the Novels of Margaret Atwood*. Amherst: U of Massachusetts P, 1993.

Gorjup, Branko. "Margaret Atwood's Poetry and Poetics," *The Cambridge Companion to Margaret Atwood*. Coral Ann Howells, ed. Cambridge: CUP, 2006.

Grace, Sherrill. *Violent Duality: A Study of Margaret Atwood*. Montreal: Vehicule Press, 1980.

Howells, Coral Ann, ed. *The Cambridge Companion to Margaret Atwood*. Cambridge: CUP, 2006.

_____. "On the Border: Margaret Atwood's Novels," *Bloom's Modern Critical Views: Margaret Atwood*. Harold Bloom, ed. New York: Infobase, 2009.

Tolan, Fiona. *Margaret Atwood: Feminism and Fiction*. New York: Rodopi, 2007.

# Book Review

**Ashwin Sanghi, *Keepers of the Kalchakra*, Westland Publications, 2018. 406 pp. Rs. 399**

History and myths hold a great charm for the novelists and readers in our times. That is why the re-telling of myths has become a lucrative writing business. While re-telling a myth or epic story, the writers have been seen to adopt different strategies. It could be a faithful re-telling in modern English language with writer's own contribution standing out clearly as is the case with Devdutt Pattnaik's writings. It can also be a re-representation with varying degrees of moulding of the original storyline. From Ashok Banker to Amish Tripathi to Ashwin Sanghi, this allegiance to the original story has been weakening, so that in the last named, the link with the original storyline becomes rather tenuous.

Sanghi takes up only a historical or mythical icon as the starting point and then goes at a tangent fabricating his own stories with an unbelievably large number of ingredients like science, myth, history, politics, human psychology, anthropology and what not. Sanghi made his debut with *The Krishna Key,* which shows a murderer who believes himself to be Kalki—the final Kalyugi incarnation of Lord Vishnu—who has the right to punish the guilty. His other novel *Chanakya's Chant* created a story on the lines of the story of Chanakya who taught Chandragupta Maurya, the ruler of Magadh empire. It is only that the author dubs his protagonist as the reincarnation of the historical Chanakya.

Sanghi's latest thriller, *Keepers of the Kalachakra,* bears the title which has reference to the Buddhist concept of time—both this-worldly and the celestial. He is a pioneer in the craft of mingling epic details with bits of history, science, current events, to create an interesting thriller of a unique kind. The novel has substantial portion devoted to the description of development of religion and science, even as the treatment is not entirely factual. Sanghi's book has diagrams, pictures, to make the narration intelligent. But some thrilling details like self-mummification by Buddhist monks (134) can't vouchasafe its veracity. There are also hearsay, as for example, peacocks not dying from poison but getting a brighter glint on their plumes (131).

The story of the novel proceeds as in a science thriller. Several world leaders are dying of a mystery disease which becomes the chief reason for the coming together of the intelligence agencies of four countries—U.S., Russia, China and India to work out the mystery. So, the Milesian Labs, located deep within the hills of Uttarakhand, is assigned the job and Vijay Sundaram, the young scientist researching quantum physics at IIT Delhi, is picked up, literally, to undertake research. While working on the project, he stumbles upon some secrets which, if not tackled in time, threaten to destroy the world. So, he races against time to save mankind from the impending doom.

Of the researchers involved, the Russian character Mikhailov is the son of an archaeologist who worked in India for a long time and so has good knowledge of its history and ancient texts. There is mention of a lake with skeletons at its bottom. He relates a story about the sages in that area having brought about a hailstorm on the head of revellers who disturbed their meditation. This was done through marshalling of the energy field lying untapped for over 700 years there. Mikhailov claims to be able to handle the energy fields himself.

Reading this kind of novel, you don't know where facts mingle with fiction, even though the writer has given some 58 references at the end of the book. In fact, the disclaimer at the beginning of the book has to be prioritized over the Bibliography at the end! In between, there are many hiatuses in the narrative, which are devoted to discussions on issues like the birth of various religions—Hinduism, Buddhism, Islam, Taoism—and their record over ages, particularly with regard to violence. The characters and locations belong to various regions of the world.

Sanghi also incorporates many mystical concepts along with scientific theorems, historical incidents and conspiracy theories. Again, as in a postmodern text, time and space are conflated so that real life personages like the Dalai Lama co-exist in this novel with the ageless sanyasi Brahmanand who can appear and disappear at will. Scientific explanations are juxtaposed oddly with a lot of mumbo-jumbo, whimsical graphics, etc. So do current historical details like the occupation of Tibet by China with what happened when Nalanda was destroyed long back.

Characters discuss philosophies like the concept of Brahman as evidenced in Buddhism (*dharmakya*) and Taoism (*Tao*) while Sanghi locates modern physics in the Rig Veda, Buddhist sutras, and Sufism of Ibn Arabi. There are stories ascribed to different nations as far apart as America and Syria, or Russia and Australia. The narrative—a collage of episodes and discussions—straddles theories of quantum physics, concept of historical time, religious philosophy, business practices and contemporary politics, and it requires some determined suspension of disbelief to enjoy this mish-mash! This suspension will perhaps be easier in the case of an ordinary reader when he reads the explanations regarding the period of *Ramayana* or the building of Ram Setu bridge. (42)

It must, however, be added that Sanghi is ruthless in pointing out the flip side of all religions. If he condemns Hindu text *Manusmriti* for favouring oppressive casteism, he also criticizes

Christianity, quoting from the Bible to show that God wanted followers to come down heavily on the non-believers. In the same vein, he claims that Sikh texts have been misused to justify terrorism to support the Khalistan movement and Jainism permits people to starve themselves to death.

While taking up Islam, he finds two things different. While the adherents of other faiths do not take religious texts literally, and are able to differentiate between religion and state, the followers of Islam do not do so. And that leads to support for terrorism: "Ordinary Muslims see the lack of separation between religion and state as a weakness. But terrorists see that as their strength. They know that an effective army is not that questions why. It is one that obeys commands." But then Sanghi forgets that even among Islamic scholars, there is a section that interprets the Sharia to mean no support for terror. The book, however, ends with the suggestion that "Maybe the time for Islamic reformation has arrived?" (401). On the whole, it is a riveting novel indeed!

**O.P. Jindal Global University, Sonepat JAGDISH BATRA**

# Creative Writing

## The Fruit

Grafted to a mango tree, the creeper
of a cucumber yields cucumbers
all pristine traits well preserved.
My social foe attributes
'Mangoism' to the cucumber!
Colour-blinded? Blind-coloured?
A morose sleep? A pose to feign probity?
Mono-long-legged yoga? For so too long!?
I did careen to the side of the One
who fixedly stretched out His hands
for I couldn't stretch mine towards
the dregs and the crud of the world,
cringe and touch the untouchable.
Thus I grafted my caste to the Cross
since it has no 'touch' criterion.
The *persona grata* curbed my legal leeway
Blazoning to the world:
'Poverty cannot touch the Faith'
with an implicit ruling that I die in penury.
Crawling on belly and knowing its value,
Manu's muckraking quadruped monster
cavorts about a foxtrot on my gut.
The eye is the crucial sensory perception,
and the eye-tied 'goddess of justice'
cannot be an audience to the obloquy.
What a handicap! What a handicraft!

I bitterly tore off my caste deed into pieces,
And cast them on the flinty head of felony,
for it only serves as a mere official proof
of snide and venal polity of fanatic fawners.
That's it. Ever since,
the rich ruby red ambrosia of the Cross
has been flooding my life with
manifold blessings for generations.
What a miracle! The story of grafting
has taken a unique turn this time
yielding myriads of fruits of the Cross in me.

## The Answer

I met him on the first avenue
And asked him, "Why do you despise me?"
He chanted, "You live on the fifth avenue."
I met him on the second avenue
And asked him, "What's my mistake?"
He roared like a lion, "You aren't muscled."
I met him on the third avenue
And asked him, "Why do you reject me?"
He calculatedly said, "You have no money."
I met him on the fourth avenue
And asked him, "Why am I not accepted?"
He jeered at me, "You are unfit even to serve."
I met my own neighbour on the "fifth avenue"
And asked him, "What wrong have I done?"
He sneered, "You are my contender."
Then He came to me from the Seventh Avenue
And I wept, "Who do I belong to?"
Wiping my tears, He said, "You are Mine."

**The Light**

In my drowse, it ignites ire in me
if my eyes encounter light.
Until it's smothered, a wink of sleep
outdoes a raindrop in a fiery summer.
When the Son rose as the Sun,
my world was dozing in sin.
Mulish with the notoriety of Edenic tort,
filled with brazen nude blindness,
I found the Light of the world odious.
The glut of the stupor of sin in me
possessed my cult and will, and
coarsely doused the trans-terrene Light.
The sopor reigned supreme, lulled by night.
The triune God lit up the lamp
again on the third day
to spread aurora all over the universe
with neither extinction nor repression.
If I close my eyes for the last time
before I see the morn of the sun?
No, it will be sooty—utterly aphotic—
even if a ritual lamp is lit
at the head of my corpse.
May the light fully irradiate
the dusky room of my soul!
May I brightly shine in the world and
illumine the path of the soon coming King!

**Praveen Dasari**
**Andhra Loyola College, Vijayawada**

## All in an Inebriated State

Vasan in the prime of his youth and Mohan his father,
Strange enough, were habitual inseparable alcoholics,
What they earned by the sweat of their brows
From dawn to dusk was drained away at night,
They sat in the TASMAC and boozed happily.
They caroused as long as their purses were fat
And there was a passage in their throats,
They returned home tottering and rubbing shoulders.
Time came for them to steep in the 'death of each day's life.'

The only cot in their house became the bone of contention,
Each of them strove hard to lie on the single cot.
A flimsy reason gave rise to a grave problem.
Who will occupy the cot and who will lay head
On the mat on the floor, that was the question.
Before the decision was taken, the son in haste took
The liberty of laying his limbs on the cot.
Mohan viewed it seriously and vied with Vasan
To use the cot but in vain, for Vasan was as dead as wood.

Mohan in a fit of fury hit his son with a rod.
Vasan's groaning awoke the neighbours who rushed
Him to the nearby hospital where he died.
Law showed its face and justice was rendered
The son is in the grave to rest in peace
And the sire is in prison to brood over his fate.
Our benign govt is very proud of the proceeds from its TASMAC.

We are reminded of the Holy verse
"Nations will rise against nations.
Sons will rise against sires and the vice versa."
Besides this, sore famines, earthquakes and plagues
Augur the end of the world and herald His second coming.

**G. Maria Joseph Xavier, Madurai**

**Krishna!**

The Son . . .
Affection and care personified
Karmic bond eternalized

The Friend . . .
Confidant and mentor
Trust and concern galore

The Guru . . .
Pacifier of the storm
Renderer of the calm

The Saviour
Insightful Faith Healer
Angelic life-saver

**Sumita Puri**
**Dyal Singh College, University of Delhi**

## Comet Stalking

Pan STARRS
What a mundane name
for a heavenly happening!

Have you seen it yet?
It proves to be as elusive
as the infamous Pacific green flash
stalked by Waikiki tourists over Barber's Point
the happiness stalked by me,
fleeting streaks of bright light
that shoot out of my grasping hands.

Does it streak? Or drop?
Lead? Or stop?
Find its way over a stable
Or a grave?

What are you a harbinger of?
A tragedy of Shakespearean proportions
The death of man, a marriage, a life
The fall of a magnanimous?
Or a messenger of good luck?
Mercurian or Jupiterian?

Can I catch you and save you
In my pocket, like a Pleaidian falling star
Will you grant a wish,
or will you elude me still?

Will you respond to me
Rapidly?

**Fractured**

A purple pensiveness
falls over me, as I
contemplate
fractured bodies
and purple passions.

Who will love me now,
at sixty-six,
with lumpectomied
one and half breasts
and a bulging
inguinal hernia
caused by
moving boxes
after the radical hysterectomy
of cancer past.

None will hold women
broken and fragmented
afraid to touch
cracked glass,
like shards of crystal glassware
dropped in the deliberate abandonment
of betrayals, wrought
by callous men.

Why do we submit?
to fracturing?

Grief is painful to contemplate
In purple pensiveness.

**Elegy for My Trees**

The weather is turning;
not, as it usually does,
when liquid gold
comes and goes,
dripping from amber branches
that shed their emerald ear drops.

This year there is no crunch
to the gold dried to airy thinness.
It is soggy damp. Slippery and sliding,
causing falls.

The skies have been weeping,
Filling the ever overflowing rain barrels.

The continuous damp chill,
has wilted my Afghan pines
traumatized by the drought
in and around me, unready for this
bounty of water.

Many years of dry drought
have not prepared, desert sand or bark,
to absorb
what should be a gift of rain.

Instead, damp bark leeches water
releasing pine beetles, for
busy woodpecker heads to
peck, peck, peck,
tap, tap, tap.

It is a wonder their little heads don't
fall off,
similarly making them fodder
for the lone hawk that sits
on his dying throne
a throne that I must soon have felled
before it tumbles and crumbles.

No, this water has not been a blessing,
as it breaks the banks of rivers
used to dry edges:
"This is how we were meant to be," they say,
"to be streams in a desert,
For, when we are full and flush,
greedy gold diggers, mistaken mine cleaners,
break veins, that loose
poison into our life blood."

Petrichor turns to putrifacation,
as drowning roots, lose loose soil
threatening to topple
stately majestics that must be felled
before canyon winds blow them over.

No, we have abused mother earth too long,
and now she lets loose wind and weather,
tides that bring in the *amakua*, as sharks
that bite children by the seaside.
This niño does not bring a blessing,

Santo Niño, can you save us with your rebirth?

**Feroza Jussawalla**
**University of New Mexico, U.S.A.**